David Niethe is a mental-performance coach with a unique approach. His philosophy has helped athletes, coaches, managers, business owners, CEOs and students develop the skills and mindset to create a fearless mentality, reframe failure and remove self-limiting beliefs.

David has worked with some of the world's most talented athletes including golfer Lydia Ko and MMA fighter Israel Adesanya.

He is based in Auckland, New Zealand.

THE WINNING MINDSET

David Niethe

HarperCollinsPublishers

HarperCollins*Publishers*
Australia • Brazil • Canada • France • Germany • Holland • India
Italy • Japan • Mexico • New Zealand • Poland • Spain • Sweden
Switzerland • United Kingdom • United States of America

First published in 2024
by HarperCollins*Publishers* (New Zealand) Limited
Unit D1, 63 Apollo Drive, Rosedale, Auckland 0632, New Zealand
harpercollins.co.nz

HarperCollins*Publishers*
Macken House, 39/40 Mayor Street Upper
Dublin 1, D01 C9W8, Ireland

A catalogue record for this book is available from the National Library of New Zealand

ISBN 978 1 7755 4247 6 (paperback)
ISBN 978 1 7754 9278 8 (ebook)

Cover design by HarperCollins Design Studio
Cover image by Haley Guildford
Illustrations by Saachi Owen
Typeset in Adobe Garamond Pro by Kirby Jones

Printed and bound in the United States

For Jo

Contents

INTRODUCTION

What is the winning mindset?

It's what sets apart the people who go on to achieve greatness, whether in the sporting arena, the business world or within their personal lives. These people have been able to look directly into the things they fear and, ultimately, overcome them. By shining a light on their values, beliefs, goals, language and perceptions, their self-image has become stronger and they've set themselves free.

There is something beautiful in building a strong self-image. Through the process of gaining that winning mindset, you will become fearless and be able to endure any feedback or criticism without it affecting your belief in yourself.

You will even learn to reframe failure. I've worked as a mental-performance coach for the last 30 years, working with some of the finest athletes in New Zealand and around the world. I've helped to produce champions consistently over that time and I guarantee that, if you're on the journey to high success, you will pass through failure many times. You can let this define you, or you can use it as energy to keep moving forward.

I describe myself as a 'meat and potatoes' coach with a simple approach to helping people be the most successful versions of themselves.

I work on the basis that having a brain is a bit like having a car: you don't need to know how it works, you just need to know how to drive it. It's about empowering people by telling them that they're in the driver's seat and change is in their hands.

In today's world, resilience is important, but how do you develop it? What does it look like? In this book, I will share simple strategies to help you understand and build resilience. It can be challenging, but everyone has the capacity to make change. Let's start with a promise that you'll be blunt and honest with yourself; that is the key to opening your mind to the winning mindset and becoming your best self.

I'm not academically inclined; I'm a blue-collar worker who has overcome a lot of things and been through a lot of stuff. I'm really proud of how I managed to get to where I am. My words and actions match each other, and I know that's what people like about working with me. I am comfortable with my authoritative style because I've done the work; I've had the experience, knowledge and wisdom to help create change.

Dealing with people is a huge responsibility. Mine is a no-bullshit approach and I am not for everyone. I get that. I'm not here to be your friend, I'm here to help you perform. If you're prepared to put in the time and effort, and are willing to be honest and blunt with yourself, my advice will work for you too. When you nail the winning mindset, understand it and apply it, you'll see and feel the evidence constantly in your world.

There is no 10-step programme that's going to create the life you want: the process is more of a wonderful journey. I can't definitively say, 'You must do this, then this, then this.' I can offer guidance, but within that there's flexibility – the key thing is to build momentum. A lot of what you need will be worked out along the way, but the fact that you're moving forward is what's important. You need to be able to say, 'I'm moving towards something.'

My story

When I was growing up in the 1970s, my parents always worked hard. My old man worked six days a week in the printing industry and mum worked two jobs to make ends meet. Because they worked such long hours, I used to go to Grandma and Grandad's house on the way home from school every day. There, Grandma would always have a canvas on her easel so we could paint together. She also always had the biggest container of biscuits, which was a real treat for a young lad.

Grandad had served in the Royal Air Force. He married my grandma after the Second World War and they started their married life in Germany, where he was stationed for a couple of years.

By the end of their time in post-war Germany, they just wanted to start afresh. What better way to do it than to move somewhere that didn't need to be rebuilt? New Zealand's economy was booming and workers were needed, so there was a scheme encouraging young Brits to move over. By the time my grandparents arrived, my grandmother's brother – Uncle John – was already here.

For a while Grandad worked at a power station down country, then they moved up to Papakura, which was a relatively new suburb at the time. Uncle John did a couple of security jobs before he and Grandma opened a jewellery shop in Papakura. They later opened a second one in Papatoetoe.

Uncle John was a fine, handsome man and a career soldier. During the Second World War, he served as a tank commander in North Africa. As a kid, I used to sneak into his room, put on his uniform, grab his Enfield rifle and pretend to shoot bad guys.

My grandad and Uncle John were very influential in my life. Grandad had tremendous charisma and rapport with people. He was a talented man. Uncle John was very regimented and was a military man through and through. In my office today, I have photos of Grandad and Uncle John taken during their time in the military, to remind me of their courage, every day. I think I owe some of my tenacity to Grandma, Grandad and Uncle John. They were my heroes and I miss them dearly. I was lucky to have time with them growing up.

Even after having us kids, Mum continued to work at the jewellery shop during the day. She'd come home and cook our dinner, then at night she'd go to a factory and pack biscuits. She used to bring home boxes of offcuts, which I loved! Weirdly, biscuits would later play a role in one of the most defining moments in my life.

After our family moved out to Hunua, I spent a lot of time playing rugby league in muddy paddocks with my mates and going hunting for rabbits and possums. While life there was fantastic for me and my brother and sister, things were challenging for my parents, as high interest rates caused them financial stress.

At the age of 13, I was sent to boarding school at Wesley College in Pukekohe. Back then, quite a lot of bullying took place, and it wasn't long before one of the older boys started on me. He stole food from me and beat me up every chance he got.

I was less upset by getting beaten up than by how scared and powerless it made me feel.

After a few hidings, I finally decided to stand up for myself. The decision was triggered by a parcel that arrived for me from Uncle John, containing a bag of Farmbake cookies. Whenever we got tuck, the bigger guys would come and grab whatever us smaller guys had been sent. I knew what was about to happen and I thought about my Uncle John, who was my hero. I loved listening to his stories about things he'd been through in the war. I saw him as a really strong person, who wouldn't put up with nonsense from anyone. It was then that I realised I'd had enough of being beaten up and stolen from.

When the older guy came up to me, grabbed me and said, 'Give me your fuckin' biscuits,' I decided that I wasn't going to put up with it anymore.

Instead of just handing them over, I said, 'No, fuck off, they're mine.'

He moved closer. I made a fist and pummelled this guy on the chin with everything I had, which was like a tiny mosquito bite to him. His expression of surprise was priceless. He called me names and proceeded to give me a hiding – but he never touched me again.

I stood up for myself, and that triggered something in me that has continued to grow to this day: a desire to be fearless.

It made me wonder, *If I have the guts to do that, what else can I do?*

There was another thing that happened at school that changed my life. It was there that I met Reverend Graham Kane, a fantastic guy. Though Wesley College was Methodist, for him it wasn't about pushing God. He was more like a personal development coach.

He gave me a copy of the book *Jonathan Livingston Seagull.* I read it and thought, *Jonathan's me and I am Jonathan!* That helped trigger this whole, wonderful journey of wanting to be fearless. I'm still on that journey and I will continue it forever.

The promise I made off the back of these events was that I didn't want to be bullied and I didn't want to be a bully. I would be assertive and pull people up if they disrespected me.

One of the strange things about having been bullied is that, in hindsight, if I could change it, I wouldn't. It was terrible, but it was also a gift because it made me who I am today. I reframed the experience and used it to start on the journey of change.

Initially, the change I experienced was physical. I thought, *So I'm never bullied again, I'm determined to be the biggest, strongest motherf*cker in this country*, and I became obsessed with that. I transitioned from rowing and playing rugby to competing in New Zealand Strongman. I pulled trucks, carried anvils, flipped tyres, pressed weights above my head and all that stuff, and I absolutely loved it. I even set records.

If ever there's a way to measure that you've overcome, in a sense of physical strength, it's in competing to become New Zealand's strongest man. That was the ultimate affirmation for me. I never won it, but I placed and I was really proud of that. I was also proud that I did it drug free.

On that journey, I tuned into the mental side of things. I was really interested in how far I could challenge my body physically, and I realised the only way to push it physically was to push it mentally.

I'm tenacious and I dislike coming second – I like winning! That drive is how I became obsessed with personal development, psychology and related ideas, an obsession that continues to this day. I've had 35 years of that same burning desire to learn more.

At the time, the Russians were doing some really interesting things in terms of mental strength. When I found out they were using hypnosis, I looked into how that might help me achieve more. When I started this research, there wasn't a lot of information out there about mental strength. However, I soon found authors like Jim Rohn, Dale Carnegie, Stephen Covey and Richard Bandler.

Once I got into it, I read anything I could get my hands on – things like George Clason's *The Richest Man in Babylon* – and whatever audio I could find, especially if it was by Earl

Nightingale, whose *Lead the Field* and *Our Changing World* were hugely popular. These guys inspired me and I became obsessed with myself as my ultimate project as a result. As I went through this process for myself, I realised that self-improvement was my thing.

By this time I'd left school, having failed School Certificate in fifth form (the equivalent of Year 10) and gone back to do it again. Doing the year over just confirmed what I felt already: I hated school. My self-image at that time was that I was dumb. I'd failed every subject.

The old man pulled some strings and got me an apprenticeship at a printing company. Each week we pumped out women's magazines, and I couldn't have been less interested. The job was miles away from what someone with my personality should have been doing, but I didn't know any better. I hated the job.

At one point, I thought I might join the police. I knew I'd pass the physical, but the written part – not so much. While I was working towards doing the entrance exam I met this wonderful lady who took me aside and said, 'I want to run some tests.' She told me I had dyslexia and gave me some tips on how to read and practise writing more effectively.

No wonder I'd had trouble at school! There I was, dyslexic and doubting my intelligence.

In a sense, having the diagnosis freed me. I decided almost immediately that I wasn't going to comply with all of the things that having the label 'dyslexic' meant. I wanted to attack and overcome. It was like anything in life: in order to improve my reading and writing, I had to practise.

My investigation and curiosity were also sparked by the diagnosis. I'm still like an eager kid when it comes to learning new things, and I hope that energy never leaves me.

I became even more determined to understand mental performance. When I realised how much I loved it, I had this dream of doing it full time as a job. I started to see the possibility – even though it was a very faint one – of having a career as some sort of mental-skills coach.

Meanwhile, I was still helping pump out magazines as a printer. One day a manager came along and said, 'Hey, Dave, what's this bullshit about you doing this motivational psychology stuff? Mate, you only just managed to pass your apprenticeship.'

That hurt. My self-belief was challenged, so my internal dialogue began to say: *Do you believe in yourself? Getting into psychology? I mean, come on. That's for intellectuals.*

I stood there looking at this guy who had just belittled me. I didn't know how to respond to him, so I didn't. What I did, though, was use his words as fuel.

One night, I was watching TV and feeling frustrated with life when I saw an advertisement for some tapes by a motivational speaker. I immediately got excited and ordered them straight away, then spent hours listening to them.

I'm not saying the path ahead was suddenly clear and everything was fine, but I knew that this was the information I needed if I was to have any chance of owning my own life.

I figured a job in a different country would get me out of where I was, which would be a start. I convinced myself there was nothing left for me in Auckland (which absolutely was not true), so I applied for a job with a print company in Sydney. They sent a guy over to Auckland to do the interview. Afterwards he shook my hand and said, 'Mate, we'll get the contract through to you.'

That was it – I was off!

I told my flatmate that we were going out to celebrate my new job. He reminded me that he'd answered a 'flatmates wanted' ad in the local newspaper and we were supposed to be going around to look at the place that evening.

I said, 'I don't think so, mate. We're getting on the piss! I got the job and I'm off to Aussie. I'll be earning a lot more money there!'

My flatmate nagged at me to go and look at this place. Reluctantly, I agreed to go with him. We showed up late, and the moment Jo opened the door, I knew I wasn't going to Sydney.

I moved in, and Jo and I flirted like crazy. There was just something about her. She was a real free spirit. She was stubborn and determined, and she was loving and caring – just a beautiful soul. We became a couple soon after, and we've been together ever since. It's been a really easy relationship. We still live in that same house, and over the years we've created our own private paradise. We've also become a family with our two wonderful children, Maddison and Mitchell. I'm so proud of them both.

Living across the road was a man called Clive Littin, who became my first coach and mentor. Clive was quite tough on me, but I loved every minute of working with him. Clive's knowledge of therapy and understanding of people was amazing, and he shared with me all he'd learned through his years of study. As we sat in his beautiful garden, I felt so empowered. He was all about accountability and goal setting. He was brilliant. I often talk about the importance of valuing things and the idea that, in order to value something, sometimes you have to struggle.

When I saw Clive, he charged $80 an hour. I was a printer with a mortgage, earning $7 an hour. I used to have to work overtime to save up enough for an hour with Clive, but because I worked so hard, I valued that time with him. I was like a sponge.

Soon, I was confident and eager to leave my printing job. I was determined to build my own coaching business. I needed to do it step by step. Doing shift work meant I could never establish my own business, so first I got a print sales job, which meant I could work nine to five, five days a week. This allowed me to use my nights and weekends to focus on my own goals. I started coaching a few clients and slowly built my own business as a sideline before taking the leap and going full-time.

I was very lucky to have my wife's support all the way through. Her belief in me is amazing. We risked it all, and for the first five years of this business, Jo and I struggled financially. Back in the late 1990s, mental-skills coaching wasn't even a thing. No one talked about mental performance back then. I'm quite proud that it's something I've helped pioneer in this country. It was challenging work, but I had to push through.

Even though I've been doing this for 30 years, I'm only now beginning to feel like I'm doing some really good work. I'm loving this ongoing journey.

In eliciting change in people, I believe that success requires one thing, and if you don't have it, you might as well give up. That one thing you need? 100 trillion cells. We're all made up of the same number of cells, so everyone has within them everything they need to make change, but that has to be backed with tenacity, vision, discipline and self-awareness.

Nietheisms

Throughout this process, you're going to hear several phrases repeated. There will be concepts that come up again and again, and they each reinforce each other. They are applicable in lots of different situations and are the keys to achieving your goals. Once you've got them anchored in, you'll be well on the way to having that winning mindset. Some to look out for are:

- Congruence*
- Protect yourself at all times
- The map is not the territory
- Divide and conquer
- Mind your language

Speaking of language, when my seminars are advertised I usually include the words, 'Language may offend.'

I am the first to admit my language is probably not appropriate, but I don't give a fuck because I think the message and the intention of the message is always to serve and to help. If all people hear is my swearing, they're listening for the wrong thing.

* I believe it's important for me to be able to live the way I'm telling others to live, and that I follow the principles I give my clients. That's what I mean when I use the word 'congruence' – there's a match between what I say and what I do.

Chapter 1

IF IT'S GOING TO BE, IT'S UP TO ME

Life by design, not default

Do you give me permission to be blunt and honest with you?

That's one of the first questions I ask my clients when they come to see me. Most of the time, my clients are fully aware of what they want. They have big goals, things they really want to achieve, but there are obstacles standing in their way. What a lot of people don't realise is that the main thing preventing them from achieving their goals is them.

We can't tiptoe around the fact that, whether we like it or not, everyone has to take responsibility for themselves. You are exactly where you should be in life right now, due to the sum of the thoughts and the actions that you've taken.

I get it. Sometimes it's uncomfortable to face up to things that you don't want to think about. The ego gets in the way. People are very good at creating their own victim story and then getting other people to reinforce it. That's why it's so important for me to ask for permission to be blunt and honest, so I can get through whatever stories people are telling about themselves and work with them to make meaningful change.

I'm not a counsellor. I'm a mental performance coach. What I do is about challenging people – challenging them to understand their values, identify their goals, understand the beliefs they hold that limit them and then help them to become consciously aware while they build a strong self-image.

Become something more than what you were

Uncle John and Grandad both served in the Second World War and they used to talk to me about their experiences. Since then, I've always had this mindset that, out of respect for the men and women who gave their lives for our freedom, each and every one of us has a responsibility to be the best we can and all we can be. If everyone had that mentality, I think this world would be a better place. This idea challenges us to take responsibility, to look at our vulnerabilities and investigate them, and to overcome.

The idea of being the best you can be is open to each person's interpretation. I remember making a promise to myself that I never wanted to be *a* coach, I always wanted to be *the* coach. That was the commitment I made to myself. It wasn't from an arrogant perspective; it was about consistently being the best version of myself in that role.

How did I define being *the* coach back then? I'm not sure, but what mattered was taking on the accountability. That goal helped hold me to account, to be congruent and to be continuously educating myself. Now if I'm talking to a group of young people I'll say, 'If you're going to be an electrician, I don't want you to be just any electrician. If you're going to be a nurse, I don't want you to be just any nurse. I want you to be *the* electrician or *the* nurse.'

The most incredible project you will ever undertake is you. The most incredible gift you will ever be given is your life. You have an opportunity to go and create the best version of you.

Life by design

One of the sayings I really love is, 'If it's going to be it's up to me.'

Too many people live life by *default*, and that's a big mistake. Instead, we should be taking control and living life by *design*.

For the last 30 years – since I made the choice to live life by design – I don't set an alarm clock. Sure, I will if I have to get to the airport or something, but otherwise, no. I love that, because for a period of my life, from the age of 16 to 23, I lived life by default. I spent my life clocking in on someone else's schedule because that's what I thought was expected of me.

Now I like to ease into the day, have breakfast with my wife. My whole life is designed to work for me.

If you're self-employed or you want to be, it's important to work out your non-negotiables and then stick to them.

My creative process happens within the time I'm engaging with clients. It's an intuitive process. That can be quite draining, so I need to protect my downtime so I can recharge and do it all again. That said, a lot of the time, what I do doesn't feel like work because I have the privilege of sitting down with like-minded individuals, having intellectual conversations. How cool is that?

Part of living life by design is that, in each and every moment of the day, I have the opportunity to make a decision. I try to make decisions that will improve the probability of a positive outcome.

Nothing's guaranteed. If you can accept that and work within that, it can then put you at ease to focus on what you can control and get the most out of life.

Pain is unavoidable

Most people think that in order to be happy they have to avoid pain. However, there will always be challenges and difficulties. The blessing of going through pain is that it helps us to appreciate the happiness we have. How can you appreciate happiness if you don't have a frame of reference? It's like night and day, summer and winter.

If you lived a life of happiness all the time, you wouldn't know that you *were* happy, because you wouldn't know anything else.

When you experience frustration, fear or failure, the key thing is to preserve the lessons and let go of the negative emotions. Focus on the question, *What can I learn from this? What can I gather from this that will allow me to become a better person?*

I want to experience pain. I want to experience frustration. Pain and frustration are the biggest teachers in life. I see them as being like the light from a lighthouse: they help guide you and they remind you of your purpose. Sometimes, they're a blessing – even if they don't feel like it at the time. Sometimes a painful experience, like a redundancy or a relationship break-up, can lead to even greater things.

Fundamentally, pain is a great motivator. It means new life, yet people fear it.

The motivational filtering system

Every person is somewhere on this scale when it comes to motivation to change:

1. Moving away from pain.
2. Comfortable in the middle.
3. Moving towards something.

Out of the two movement options – away from or towards – wanting to move away from pain is the more powerful when it comes to the power of motivation. People will do anything to get away from pain. It's a big motivator.

In the middle and comfortable can be the most dangerous place because there's no motivation to move – and that's where most people sit. We're good at compromising on our goals because we're comfortable. If you're in that middle space, the likelihood is you're living life by default rather than design. That said, there's got to be a certain amount of comfort in how you organise your life. You can be physically comfortable, but you should always seek to challenge yourself to become the best version of you.

In my life, I've moved away from the pain of a job that I hated to create what I have now. That's why I'm comfortable. However, I've never lost sight of that motivational filtering system. I ensure that I am constantly moving towards something. Where my pain, fear or attention lies tells me where I need to move towards.

I tell some of my athletes, 'We've got to seek pain. Pain is beautiful. Reframe it! Pain means new life.'

You're not going to avoid pain. You learn to really understand that. You need to learn to embrace it as a reality of life. By reframing pain, you can use it to motivate you to continue moving towards whatever it is that you want out of life.

The victim's story

In society today, people do everything they can to avoid pain. That's why they make excuses – because they fear the consequences that might come from taking responsibility for their actions. That's why they don't take ownership of their lives and their decisions, because taking ownership might mean they have to see things that cause them pain. They end up becoming stuck.

When you operate from cause and not effect, that's freedom. Saying, 'I caused this' might be a hard pill to swallow sometimes, but it will set you free.

Stop blaming society, your family, your boss … whoever. Those things can impact your life – absolutely – but I still believe that you are the only one who can make meaningful change, and you do that by taking responsibility.

Yes, there are people who are brought up in very challenging situations. I totally acknowledge that, and it can be difficult, but there are plenty of examples of people who have overcome.

I love the story of Chi-Chi Rodriquez. He was born in a slum in Puerto Rico, and as his family struggled to make ends meet, he saw a bunch of Americans playing golf. He realised their caddies were making a lot of money, so he decided to become a caddy.

He was smart enough to recognise that learning to hit that little white ball around would earn him even more money. Before he had even turned 10, he carved himself a golf club out of a tree branch and started hitting tin cans with it. He turned pro when he was 25, and he went on to win eight PGA tour events.

A lot of people lean on their backgrounds and their early lives to give themselves an excuse not to achieve. That's why I ask, 'What's your victim story?' For me, it could so easily have been 'I was bullied at school' or 'I have dyslexia', but I chose not to let either of those things define my future.

When I hear people repeating their victim story, I'll always call them on it. It's too easy to stay in that story, and if you stay there, you'll never achieve your potential. If, instead of staying comfortable in that space, you decide to set some goals and move towards something new, the positive change you can create in your life is immeasurable. These goals don't have to be magnificent – they can be as simple as reading an inspiring book, or going for a walk and listening to a podcast.

We work so hard to avoid trauma, to avoid pain, and yet pain is a gift. To expect life to be perfect is delusional. It is inevitable that you will have pain.

Unfortunately, a lot of people get stuck in that pain and start creating their victim story, and that's where they stay. Others see life for what it is; they realise the importance of having a purpose in life, and that puts them on a path. Why is it that some people get stuck in the trauma and others start making change?

People put more time and effort into creating and supporting their victim story than they do on creating life as they want to live it. What's sad is that, today, there's constant affirmation of that. Everyone's going, 'Oh, poor you.' I've lost count of the number of times I've had clients come who've clearly worked for years on their victim story. Within 30 seconds, I'll challenge that by asking, 'Is that working for you?' then follow up with, 'If you couldn't fail, what would you do?'

Once they start to engage with a different way of thinking, I soon see a physiological change – they'll sit up straighter, they'll look me in the eye more readily – and when they really get it, they tell me that they hadn't realised what they were doing. No one realises that they're investing so much time in their victim story until they are honest with themselves, or until they give someone else permission to be honest with them.

Until you recognise that there's something blocking your way, you can't be released from it. You cannot change anything you don't first recognise.

EXERCISE

What's your victim story?

Being blunt and honest with yourself, make a list of the things in your life you use as excuses not to go after your goals or to reach your full potential. These can be big and significant, or small and seemingly insignificant things – just anything you use to explain why you can't do things.

Some common examples I hear are:

I don't have enough time.
I don't have enough money.
I don't have enough talent.

Now look over this list and understand this:

You, as an agent, as an individual, are capable of rewriting the chapters of your life.

If your list includes other people's negative opinions, reframe these to serve you, and use them as fuel.

The victim's triangle

This is a model that was first presented by psychiatrist Stephen B Karpman in 1968. It recognises that in many destructive social interactions there are three players: the victim, the rescuer and the persecutor.

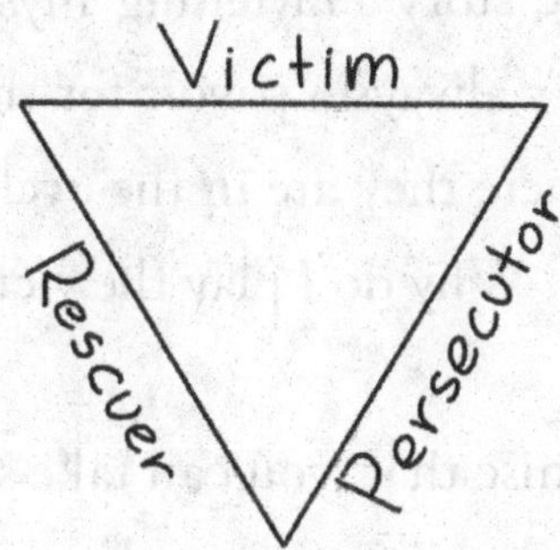

Too many people look for excuses to not do things. What do they gain by making excuses not to achieve?

Attention.

One of the biggest needs of an individual is to be affirmed and acknowledged. By creating the 'Poor me!' story, they get attention, which feels like affirmation and acknowledgement.

By doing this, they can fall into the victim's triangle. In the victim's triangle, people can play the victim, the rescuer or the persecutor, and their roles can change at any time.

They'll play the victim and people will persecute them, then others will come in and try to rescue them. Rescuing someone doesn't help them – it just perpetuates the cycle. People can spend a lot of their lives in that cycle, and it's so sad.

The most beautiful thing you can do is take the loving option, and the loving option sometimes means that you need to be blunt and honest with yourself. That can be challenging but it will set you free.

People need to ask themselves: Where am I on that victim's triangle? What's the story I'm telling myself? They need to recognise that there's always a payoff for their behaviour and ask why they are where they are in the cycle.

'I play the victim. Why do I play the victim? Because I like to be rescued.'

When you recognise that, you can take steps to get off that triangle.

Identify your values

When you're young, your family, your school and your social group are going to be your biggest influences. These environments condition us.

The German philosopher Friedrich Nietzsche talked about the transitions we go through in order to overcome this social conditioning and become the best version of ourselves.

> *Three metamorphoses of the spirit I named for you: how the spirit became a camel, and the camel a lion, and finally a child.*
> *—Friedrich Nietzsche,* Thus Spake Zarathustra

The camel says yes to society and its rules and requirements, and it can carry a heavy load. Most of us start out as a camel, just saying yes. We comply.

Some people metamorphose from a camel into a lion. The lion is at the top of the food chain. The lion breaks rules that are dictated to it. The lion has the power to say no – and that's not an easy thing to do. It takes courage to challenge the rules. But the lion doesn't *create* its own rules and values.

The final change is from the spirit of the lion to that of a child. The child has a fresh, new beginning and an opportunity to create their own values and purpose. They become their own person, clear on their identity and with the courage to move forward. To me, that is the ultimate state to be in.

In order to get there, you're going to have to go back and address some of those things you've become conditioned to. For me, some of the conditioning was, 'If you're not smart, you have to get a trade.' There was no question of me pursuing further education. Likewise, a lot of people will model their lives on the behaviour of their parents, unconscious of the fact that it could be destructive.

Suddenly, you'll go through an awakening, which sets you free and helps you to become the lion. You'll feel like you've got a little secret, with a sense of clarity that you know where you're going and you're living your life aligned with your values. This will help you to endure the discomfort you might experience along the way.

Most people will never experience this awakening, because they feel too comfortable. For some, however, a significant emotional event can be the trigger for them to re-evaluate their life and purpose.

Knowing your values so you can live by them is a contributing factor to creating what you want in your life. In order to truly design your life the way you want it to be, it's important to identify and understand your core values: they can have a huge impact on how you live.

Values are the things that are important to you and that help to guide you when making decisions. Your values will dictate the directions you take in life, yet most people find it challenging to define what theirs are, and even fewer have ever sat down and really tried to investigate them.

If your ultimate goal is to create bliss in your life, you need to take time out to understand yourself, know what your values are and align with them as best you can. Then, with clear intent, you can undertake the challenge of creating a life of your own design. It will be hard. It will be very challenging at times, and there will be moments when you question what you're doing, but the rewards are absolutely worth the effort.

So what is a value?

A value = a preference x a priority

Each person creates their own set of values by attaching priority and importance to their own set of preferences. The difference between a belief system and a value is that a value, by definition, is a preference multiplied by a priority, while a belief is something you hope is true. In other words, a value is like a belief on steroids.

From there you have a value hierarchy, and attached to each one of those values is a belief system that supports the value.

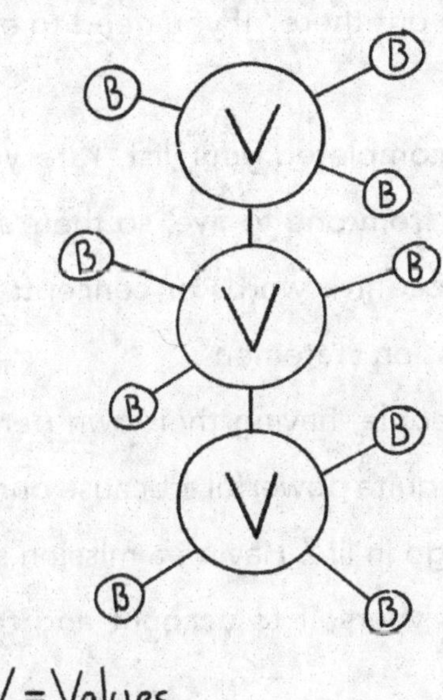

V = Values
B = Beliefs

EXERCISE

Identifying your core values and creating your personal mission statement

Make a list from 1 to 20. Alongside each number, write down something that you value.

Start each sentence with the words 'I value...'

Whatever comes into your mind, add it to the list. It might be, 'I value education', 'I value learning' or 'I value my family.' Freedom, security, faith ... there are tens of thousands of values.

Most people will do this exercise, get to about five and go, 'I might need some help here!'

I say, 'Put it all out there.' If you need to expand the list further, fire away.

Once you've completed your list, rate your five most important values from one to five, so there's a clear value hierarchy. Use those five words or concepts to build your own personal mission statement.

For a lot of people, having their own personal mission statement can be quite powerful, because our values create the direction we go in life. Having a mission statement will help you to hold yourself to account and remind you of your values.

For example, if your top five values were:

1) Balance

2) Honesty

3) Kindness

4) Time for myself

5) My friends

Your mission statement might be: 'While maintaining balance in my world, through honesty and kindness, I will make time for myself and my friends.'

When creating the mission statement, the values don't have to be listed in order. The sentence just needs to resonate with you and represent your intentions.

Once your values and mission statement have been established, it will be easier to set goals.

Your values don't have to be set in stone. Things will change and you will learn to change with them when necessary. You can revisit and change them at any time; in fact, you need to be flexible with them. They should just be a gentle guide to your decision-making. When we make a decision that aligns with our values, it should feel right.

You need to be mindful of the fact that if something *feels* right that doesn't necessarily mean that it *is* right, or that it's the right thing to do. But explicitly knowing your values should at least support a level of conviction around the decisions you make in life.

If you make decisions that align with your values, supported by a level of conviction due to understanding them, you will raise the probability of each decision moving you towards creating a life of increased happiness and bliss. If you can do that, then you're on the right track. You may not know clearly where you're heading, but you will have a sense that you're moving in the right direction.

Conflicting values

Sometimes your values may conflict with each other. If that's the case, I ask the question: 'Is there potential here for those values to change in your hierarchy, so that you can focus on one over the other for a period of time? Which of your values takes priority and which is a preference?'

I ask this question because sometimes I hear people say, 'I'm doing all the actions but I feel like there's something subconsciously sabotaging my progress.'

When I hear that sort of thing, there's usually a clash of values going on. A good example of this was an athlete I worked with who said one of their goals was to be world champion. In order to achieve this, he would have to be away from his family for long periods of time. When I went through this exercise with him, his number-one value was his family and his second one was his faith.

Going through this process enabled him to see that by being away from his family competing, he would be able to provide for them in the longer term. Although this was challenging for him, ultimately it would serve him and his family. Sometimes you have to adjust your hierarchy to serve your purpose.

Other people's values

It's also helpful to be aware that your values won't always align with those of other people. No one has the right to challenge people's values. For example, some people will put 'money' in their top five, while others place no value on it at all.

Beliefs attached to values

Refer back to your own list of values. For each one of those values, you will have certain beliefs that support or contaminate them. By definition, a belief is something we hope to be true. Ideally, each belief is there to support the value: you can consider beliefs to be the DNA of values.

Look at your circumstances, look at where you are in life. Sometimes you've got to ask yourself, 'OK, if I'm going to make dramatic change, I'm definitely going to go into my value hierarchy and think about what I can shift around.'

Now that you've looked at your values, let's start challenging some of your limiting beliefs. The key question to ask is, 'What is the story I'm telling myself?' Then follow that up with, 'Is this belief supportive of the vision and the value?'

I encourage you to really challenge your value hierarchy and the belief systems that you have around those values. This can give you a level of clarity that then allows you to create a strategy to design your life.

EXERCISE

Identifying and challenging your contaminating beliefs

Ask yourself, 'What beliefs do I currently hold that contaminate my vision or my sense of self?

Write down any of the beliefs you have that are holding you back. For example, one of my beliefs was, 'I'm not that smart.'

For every negative belief you write down, write three affirmations that counter it.

My affirmations were:

'It's easy for me to learn.'

'I get excited at the thought of learning.'

'My imagination serves me.'

My own values

When you really understand your values, that's where you get a sense of absolute clarity. My number-one value is freedom. I came from such a regimented world, and freedom allows me to make my own decisions and to live congruently. When I started living that way, I became so much happier. Prior to that my life had been really focused on security, and I was miserable.

When I met Jo, I'd gone through that change in my values and I was focused on freedom. She supported me in creating that freedom for myself. That might seem somewhat selfish, but the by-product was that Jo was also free. Our values aligned. We were both clear on what we wanted. I wanted to be the best mental skills coach I could be, and I wanted Jo to do whatever she wanted to do too.

I think you get to a point where you experience a certain level of clarity about what you want in your life. That helps you to see the value in the people you have around you. When you're not clear on what your values are, I think you're more vulnerable to manipulation, dysfunction and bad relationships.

People often question whether freedom is more important to me than family – and I can confidently tell them that it is. When I have a sense of freedom, I'm a better husband, a better dad and a better friend. That's because I'm living in congruence with my values.

Further, one of my core values is integrity in the sense of congruent coaching.

Congruence

There's no point in me sitting here telling you that you have to pursue being the best version of yourself and to live life by design if I can't do it myself. That's why you'll hear me use the word 'congruent' a lot – some people might even say that it's my favourite word!

The American Psychological Association defines congruence as:

- in agreement, harmony or conformity
- a match between psychological attributes and behaviour
- in the phenomenological personality theory of Carl Rogers, (a) the need for a therapist to act in accordance with their true feelings rather than with a stylised image of a therapist or (b) the conscious integration of an experience into the self.

Basically, what congruence means is that I will do what I say I'll do, and that what I'm asking of you isn't anything I wouldn't do or haven't done myself.

When it comes to my coaching work, congruence is absolutely vital. Coaches who are congruent are working on themselves, they're aware, they're not asking you to do something that they haven't done. I think that's important.

I've been there and done it. I've been under a 340kg squat, I've been under a 200kg bench press, I've pulled trucks, I've ripped and torn muscles, I've been bruised purple all the way down one side. I'm not afraid of the physical work, so if your goal is to become a better athlete, I know what it takes. I've spoken in front of 5000 people, I've got As on assignments at degree level, so I know what it takes to overcome core fears.

I also know what it takes to own and run my own business, to have a successful relationship, to have kids that I'm proud of and to live my life to my own design. I constantly hold myself to a higher level of accountability because I have no right to expect it from others if I can't do it myself.

PROFILE

If it's going to be, it's up to me

Jaden Movold

Wheelchair racer

- Six-time gold medallist, U20 para men, Athletics Auckland Championships, 2022
- Gold medallist, senior para men 800m and 1500m, New Zealand Track and Field Championships 2022
- Bronze medallist, open men wheelchair 400m, Australian Track and Field Championships, 2022

- Auckland University of Technology Male Athlete of the Year, 2023
- Gold medallist, senior para men 800m and 1500m, New Zealand Track and Field Championships 2023
- Bronze medallist, open men wheelchair 5000m, Australian Track and Field Championships, 2023
- Gold medallist, senior para men, 800m and 1500m, New Zealand Track and Field Championships, 2024
- New Zealand record holder for U18, U19, U20 T54 10km at time of writing
- First in 5000m T54 under-20 men's – 2023 World Para Athletics rankings

I've been working with Jaden for about two years. He's a big Breakers fan, and he heard about the work I do through them.

For a young man of only 19, Jaden has been through a lot in his life. As a result of some complex medical conditions, including spina bifida, he has spent countless days in hospital and undergone 32 surgeries so far.

Despite all of this, he's got a beautiful attitude to life. There's absolutely no 'poor me' with Jaden. Instead, he has incredible amounts of positivity and determination. That's reflected in his athletic achievements and in the work he does to change the way people view those with disabilities.

Together, we've worked on Jaden overcoming pre-competition anxiety by using visualisation, and Jaden himself says it's helped him achieve some fantastic results: 'Dave's guidance has not only led me to podium finishes and personal bests in international competitions but also led to growth in confidence and resilience.'

As well as being an incredible athlete, Jaden's also got a real cheeky side, which cracks me up. When he comes to see me, I go out to help him get his wheelchair through the doors. Every single time, he'll say, 'Ow! My leg! Jeez Dave, can you be a bit more careful!' The first time he did it, I panicked a bit. He cracked up laughing and said, 'There's no feeling in my legs, Dave...'

He's really interested in how to transfer skills from high-performance sports to life in general. He wants to use his story along with the skills he's learned through sport to inspire young kids to follow their dreams and stand up for what they believe in. He is all about resilience and positivity, so I reckon he'll be amazing at it.

Chapter 2

START WITH THE END IN MIND

Setting and testing your goals

I love it when people know what they want and where they're going. Even if their goals change, the skills that they learn will serve them for the rest of their lives. When I get a client who has curiosity about their potential improvement, my job is so much easier.

One question I always ask is, 'If you knew you couldn't fail, what would you do in your life?'

It's interesting to me that, by default, the initial response most people have to that question is, 'I don't know.'

Once they've had a little bit of time to process it, they start to come up with ideas. One idea will often spark off another, and I'll encourage that process.

The underlying concept here is that the quality of your life is directly related to the quality of the questions you ask yourself and others. Ask yourself better questions.

EXERCISE

Setting your own goals

In a quiet space, where you know you're not going to be interrupted, take some time to sit and really think about what you want to get out of this process. Give yourself permission to dream big.

Write down the answers to the following questions.

If you are already working towards a specific goal, ask yourself:

1. What is it that I want to achieve?
2. What is it that I think is stopping me from doing that?

If you are uncertain of what your goals are or what you want to achieve, ask yourself:

1. What would I do, if I knew I couldn't fail?
2. What am I really passionate about doing?

When I ask people these questions, there will be one of two responses. Either their eyes will light up and they'll know the answer immediately, or, they'll quietly say, 'I don't know.'

If you're in the 'I don't know' camp, try not to let your mind restrain you with excuses or reasons why you can't do it. Just let your mind go and follow where it takes you.

If you continue to struggle to find answers, ask yourself, 'If I did know, what would I say?'

Give yourself permission to dream big

Your goals should be as big and unrealistic as possible. In my office, I've got a hand-drawn picture of a man standing on a stage. That was my goal – that I would get up and speak in front of groups of people. That came true. It's come true so many times I've lost count – but it was a huge and completely unrealistic goal when I created that image.

A lot of people are going to disagree with you setting 'unrealistic' goals, and they might try to bring you back down to a certain level of realism. My question then is, what is it that sparks some people to say 'fuck you' and get on with reaching their goal?

I help people to identify that sort of attitude and understanding. When you're young and you have someone of authority saying to you, 'Get yourself a job', or telling you what to do with your life, you'll probably want to be compliant, because that's how we're conditioned. People want to conform because that feels like the easiest thing to do, but that can lead to them settling for a life that's less than the one they deserve.

For me, that environmental conditioning said, 'If you're smart, you go to university. If you're not smart, you get an apprenticeship.' I wasn't 'smart', so I got an apprenticeship. That's what I was taught would secure my future.

In those days, the prime focus in my value hierarchy was security. My life changed completely when I realised that *my* number one value is freedom. 'OK, I've got time on this planet and that's a gift. I'm going to put myself in a position to become the absolute best version of myself. Let's go!'

Testing your goals

Having worked out what your goals are, it's important to go through a testing process. This ensures that you've framed your goals in a way that gives you the best chance of achieving them.

Like many other coaches, I use the acronym SMART to help test goals. This process was described in an article called 'There's a S.M.A.R.T. Way to Write Management's Goals and Objectives', written by George T Doran in 1981.[1] According to Doran's principles, the acronym stands for:

- Specific
- Measurable
- Achievable
- Relevant and realistic
- Time-bound

While Doran's definition is used by most coaches, I use my own variation:

- Sensory specific
- Measurable
- Accountable
- Realistic with process, unrealistic with vision
- Timeline and deadline

Sensory specific

Be as specific as possible when you're setting your goals. The clearer you are in your language and your vision, the more likely you are to achieve the desired end result.

What this looks like is, instead of saying, 'I want to take up running', you set a more concrete goal, like, 'I want to run a marathon by this date next year.' Perhaps push yourself even further and name the marathon you'll participate in and set a time goal.

The reason for including as much information as you can is that the subconscious mind will only do just enough, so we've got to be specific about what we want. A lot of people will create a general goal that goes something like: 'I wish I had more money.' The subconscious mind will pay attention to that goal. The next time you're at the supermarket, you might find that you've got a bit of change floating around so you decide to buy yourself a lottery scratch card. When you scratch the card, you win $2.

Because you haven't been specific about what 'more money' looks like to you, your subconscious mind will see that and go, 'You said you wished you had more money – there you go! I've delivered.'

Instead, you need to be quite specific about the goal you are creating for yourself, what that looks like and how it feels. When the specific and the sensory align, it helps to improve probability of outcome. A great exercise to help you ensure your goals are specific and sensory is to create a vision board.

Vision boards

A picture is worth 1000 words. We like information, and of all the modalities, vision is the most powerful. On top of that, the process of making the board shows commitment. Having the board will continually help to ensure that you are moving towards your goal by existing as a concrete reminder. It will stop you from getting into or staying in that comfortable zone. Moving towards something takes a lot of hard work, and that's the importance of having a vision.

EXERCISE

Create your own vision board

With your goal in mind, gather together materials that represent elements of what you want to achieve. This might include magazines, printed images, maps, mocked-up newspaper reports – anything that represents your goal in a physical form.

You will also need a large piece of card, some scissors, glue and coloured pens. Depending on where you want to hang your vision board, you'll also need a suitable-sized frame and a hanging kit.

Before you start, close your eyes and ask yourself this question:

If success were a colour, what colour would it be?

Using that coloured pen, write your goal on your board in big letters.

Then use the rest of your materials to create images that represent you attaining your goal. If you've got the skills, by all means do this digitally and print out the resulting images.

Once your board is complete, hang it or place it somewhere that will ensure you see it regularly. Then it will constantly be holding you to account.

There are certain specifics that are required for the vision board to be effective. I recommend not using anything you've won in the past, like medals or certificates. When your subconscious sees those, it will think, 'Tick, won that, don't need to do any more.'

The vision board helps to hold you to account. By having it there, it serves as a constant reminder to your subconscious of what it is that you intend to achieve.

As an example, I've had a professional athlete make up a fake yearly cheque they'd written $1,000,000 on. Then they went out and achieved that.

By being specific with that goal, they started to identify as a million-dollar athlete, as opposed to someone who wanted to be a 'good' athlete or a 'good' golfer or whatever.

You're constantly programming, as the subconscious mind has no idea of the reality of time, so any thought that you continuously hold in your mind will soon seek expression through some practical means.

Your vision board helps to constantly remind you of your purpose. People who don't have purpose in life can easily become lost.

Visualisation

We understand reality through our senses. When we can see, smell, taste, hear and feel something, it becomes real to the subconscious mind, which has no idea of reality or time.

That then can have a huge impact on our behaviour, because it allows us to see and believe that achieving our goal is not only possible, but probable. Before you know it, any limiting beliefs become weaker and weaker as they're replaced with something that's far more empowering that the brain gets excited about.

Where before the brain went, 'Here's the limiting belief – I hate going to competitions because I get anxious,' now it goes, 'I love going to competitions because I get excited and I know I'm going to absolutely nail it!' That's because it's learned that excitement will give it a bigger dopamine dump than anxiety.

I worked with one team that seemed to be doing everything right but were consistently coming bottom of the table. I set them a visualisation task. Each time they arrived at practice, before they got out of the car, I asked the players to take a moment to visualise winning the final. By coming to practice with that in their minds, we created a bit of excitement and positivity, and the players all brought that important extra one per cent into the team environment. As a result, they became more competitive and their results began to change.

EXERCISE

Visualisation

Another useful way of making sure your goals are sensory specific is through visualisation. The vision board provides a visual cue, but its strength can be added to by going through a process of visualising the moment that you achieve your goal.

When I'm working with clients, I go through this process using a light form of hypnosis. However, it is possible for you to step yourself through it.

1. Find a quiet, calm, comfortable spot where you're not going to be interrupted.
2. Sit with your hands on your thighs, close your eyes and focus on your breathing.
3. Breathe in through the nose for a count of four, hold the breath for five, then breathe out slowly through your mouth.
4. Slowly, in your mind, take yourself to the moment in which you're achieving your goal. Where are you? What do you see? Who is there with you?

5. Work through each of the senses and notice what they're telling you.
   - What can you see? Notice any details – people, locations, colours
   - What can you hear? Notice any details – cheering, clapping, people congratulating you
   - What can you smell? Notice any details – chlorine, sweat, a sea breeze, food
   - What can you taste? Notice any details – a post-race drink, saliva, a celebratory cake
   - What can you feel? Notice any details – the ground beneath your feet, a medal around your neck, a cheque in your hands
6. Having taken in every last detail possible through all of your senses, slowly bring your consciousness back to being in the room. When you're ready, open your eyes.

Measurable

While your goals should be as big and unrealistic as possible, they must be reachable through a process of dividing and conquering. In other words, working with the end result in mind, you should be able to divide your ultimate goal into a series of smaller, measurable and more easily attainable goals to achieve along the way.

Once you've identified your end goal and created a vision of what it looks like, the next thing to do is ask yourself: What are the immediate steps I need to take right now to help me move towards that goal? What are the measurables? That's when you need to divide and conquer by breaking the goal down into smaller steps. These can then be further broken down into daily goals and weekly goals and so on.

By going through this process, you'll take the pressure off yourself. It's about conquering all the smaller goals along the way rather than simply focusing on the big goal.

When you work backwards, the outcome will be right there in front of you. That provides most of the energy and accountability for the behaviour required to reach the goal. You've got to be disciplined.

A lot of people will tell you that the vision doesn't matter, what matters is what you do every day. Don't get distracted by those people. Both are important, but taking little steps every day without knowing where you're going could lead you absolutely anywhere – or nowhere at all. That will not help you to increase either the possibility or the probability of your success.

Here's an example of how the process might work. Ask yourself:

What's your goal?

I want to go to the Olympics in three years' time.

What's the current qualifying standard for 100 metres women's butterfly?

57.92.

What's the current world record?

55.48.

Right, that's your target. We'll set unrealistic goals, then divide and conquer. What's your current time?

59.50.

OK, so you need to drop four seconds over the next two years. When's your next swim meet?

From there, we'll set small goals. Focusing on those smaller goals is what builds momentum, because thinking *I've got to drop four seconds off my PB and I've got training next week* is overwhelming. Instead, I'll frame it as, 'Based on the fact that you've got two years to qualify, the goal over the next four weeks is to – ideally – drop 0.2 seconds.' You're more likely to think, *I can do that.*

The quality of your performance (and life) is directly related to the quality of the questions you ask of yourself and others. In this case, it's:

How do I go about dropping that 0.2 seconds? What are the supplementary things I can work on to help make that happen?

I can fine-tune my nutrition and my recovery.

What else?

I can be a little bit clearer in my purpose and attitude at training each and every time I'm there.

All of these things are little one percenters, which in and of themselves might seem insignificant. But a one per cent improvement every day turns into 365 per cent over a year – and that's massive. That's why we divide and conquer – one per cent every day. If you continue to ask that of yourself – no, *demand* that of yourself – and hold yourself accountable, you'll achieve those goals.

It's like that old joke:

How do you eat an elephant?

One small bite at a time.

The thought of eating a whole elephant is overwhelming, whereas eating one small bite of anything at a time is much easier for your brain to comprehend.

EXERCISE

Improving possibility and probability

If you improve possibility and probability, the impact over a period of time is that you're going to accelerate towards your goals. It's about the discipline and the actions that you take constantly.

I want to ask you a simple question. Would you rather have $5 million in cash sitting on the table in front of you right now, or $1 that doubles every day for 30 days?

Don't think too hard about your answer. Then try doing the maths. Most people's initial reaction is that they'll take the lump sum.

This is a case of delayed gratification. If you go for the $1 that doubles, maybe for the first 10 days you're thinking about the $5 million and wondering if you should have taken it ... but in those last six or seven days, the money suddenly compounds. By day 30, you'll have $536,870,912.

That's a great analogy for the power of creating momentum and for the importance of making small gains consistently over a period of time.

Accountable

The traditional SMART acronym uses the word 'achievable' here. I believe that saying something has to be achievable is a cop-out – achievable for who? If you're being unrealistic with your goals and realistic with your process, being accountable is more important than someone thinking your goal is achievable.

Instead, the question to ask is, 'Who am I accountable to in order to make this happen?' I believe being accountable to yourself will set you free.

The biggest problem for some people is that, once they've set their goals, they procrastinate. My coach Clive was really big on the dangers of procrastination – someone who allows themself to procrastinate has failed to hold themself accountable. He would always say, 'You've got to put a stop to putting things off.'

I turned that into an affirmation for myself: 'You must be a do-it-now person.' Being a do-it-now person is about holding yourself accountable for every decision that you make and for doing everything in your power to reach your goals. Once you've set a goal, look upon it as an obligation. That will help you to become accountable.

Holding yourself to a high level of conscious accountability will set you free. It's also important, though, to promote and proclaim what you're doing to people you trust – good friends will help hold you to account.

This is where seeking out people who can help hold you to account is also important. Hire the experts – that's why you have good coaches, managers, nutritionists, massage therapists … whoever can help you in the process. These people will help you to gain that one per cent, while also ensuring you remain focused on your goal.

In order to be accountable, your intention and attention need to be aligned. The bottom line is we *behave* our way to success, so if the intention is right, the behaviour needs to follow.

- What are your intentions?
- Your intention is to be world champion.
- Where's your attention?
- Your attention is in the victim story, and that's why you're finding it so hard to get there.

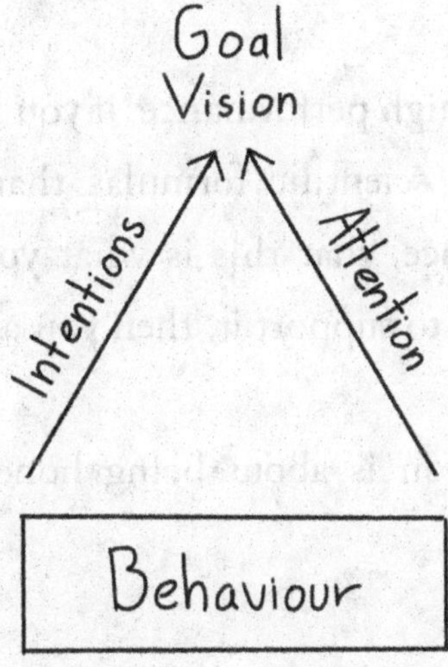

For example, if an athlete has set weight requirements they must reach in order to compete, and these requirements are made clear to them prior to their event, but they don't put the work in to meet them, then make excuses, I won't tolerate it.

The whole purpose of having a coach is so that there's someone there to hold you to account. I will point out that they have been told the requirements and I'll ask if they'd agreed to those requirements.

If they start playing the victim, I know they won't like what I have to say, but for them to have any hope of succeeding in the high-performance environment, they need to hear it.

'Immediately you were told something you didn't like, what did you do? You started playing the victim. You need to take accountability for not having done what you'd agreed to do.'

In the world of high performance, if you have requirements that are based on scientific formulas that dictate, at your peak of performance, that this is what you need to weigh, and here's the data to support it, then you are accountable for achieving that.

The loving option is about being honest. Not everyone likes that.

Realistic with process, unrealistic with vision

The traditional SMART definition here is that your goal itself has to be relevant and realistic. I say being realistic with your vision is a waste of time. I encourage people to be *unrealistic* with their vision for what they want to achieve, but to be realistic with the process they follow in order to achieve it.

Anyone that's ever achieved anything of any significance has been absolutely outrageous with their vision. That's far more exciting. No one ever says they want to be mediocre.

However, it is important that you are realistic about how you're going to make your unrealistic goal happen. Be realistic with the process, be unrealistic with the vision.

I want your goals and vision to be as big as you can make them, but in this moment – right now in the timeline – you've got to keep it real. If it's just your beliefs about your goals standing in your way, they can be dealt with. Other resources, however, may need to be taken into consideration.

Ask yourself – and be honest – do you have the time, energy, skills and any other tools that you will need in order to achieve your goal? If your answer is no, consider reprioritising the resources you do have at your disposal.

Here's an example.

What's your goal? Be as unrealistic as you like.

I want to open a restaurant that gains a Michelin star within its first year of operation.

Can you cook?

No.

Do you have any experience running a restaurant?

No.

Do you have the finance in place to open a restaurant?

No.

Do you have the time or the drive that it takes to put all those things in place within that year?

No.

It might be time to reconsider each element of that goal to make it work better for you.

Timeline and deadline

Traditionally, the T in SMART stands for time-bound. This means that it will have time-related parameters built into it. 'I will do this by 12 November 2028.'

I believe that for goals to be effective, they need to have a timeline *and* a deadline.

The timeline is important, as it will come into play when you divide and conquer and set smaller goals along the way. You can set an end date for your main goal, but smaller goals should be added to the timeline along the way.

The deadlines for each step must be absolute, so you can be held to account.

When it comes to deadlines, I'm reminded of the words of one of the great philosophers, a guy called Dirty Harry. He once said, 'A man's got to know his limitations.'

If you leave things to the last minute on a deadline, but you always deliver, that's OK. There's always a pay-off for behaviour; some people love stress because that's what holds them to account to get things done.

However, if you're prone to procrastinating, then doing the work at the last minute and not getting it up to standard, you need to start taking more accountability. It's all about working out what your optimal process is.

If you give me a test and it's an open-book test with a certain number of questions, I can be effective in doing that test. The minute you put a timeline on it, I'll struggle. I'm consciously aware of this so I know I have to be very well prepared and absolutely organised.

I've really learnt to be organised with my behaviour and structure so that when I have essays due I don't get overwhelmed with deadlines. I always have my essays done well before time because of this. It's all about the fine-tuning up to the deadline.

Too many people leave it to the last minute. If you constantly do that, it causes stress. We do need a certain amount of stress to function, but we don't want to be overwhelmed by it.

When you start to know yourself, and you know your strengths and your weaknesses, you can be better prepared for some of the challenges of life.

A tenacious resolve

On the other side of fear is a better version of you. If you've identified what you want, understand that there are going to be challenges and there are going to be moments of doubt. That's perfectly OK. What's not OK is surrendering to that. The conviction and tenacity you have and the commitment you have to the pursuit of that vision is what will get you there.

You must develop a tenacious resolve. That is absolutely crucial. When you're tenacious with the resolve to achieve the outcome, you won't need a plan B (I don't really like plan Bs). I'm a big fan of the old Viking mentality. The Vikings used to get everything on their boats – men, women, children, food, grain, everything they needed – and they'd go to a new land. When they got there they'd burn their ship because there was no turning back.

PROFILE

Building momentum

Kai Kara-France

MMA fighter

- 36 fights, 24 wins: 11 by knockout, 3 by submission, 10 by decision
- Signed to Ultimate Fighting Championship (UFC) in July 2018
- UFC Fight Night debut in December 2018 (won over Elias Garcia by unanimous decision)
- Fight of the Night winner in December 2018, September 2020, July 2022

- Performance of the Night winner 6 March 2021, December 2021
- Current ranked fourth in the UFC flyweight division
- *Caged: Kai Kara-France* documentary released in 2023

Being bullied at high school for being small was what got Kai into training (he and I have that in common). He started fighting professionally in 2010, then moved to Thailand to train in 2013. From there, he fought all over the Pacific and Asia, really putting in the hard yards to gain a UFC contract.

He first came to see me because I was working with some of the boys from City Kickboxing, one of New Zealand's most successful MMA training gyms, which is co-owned by head coach Eugene Bareman.

Kai is a great example of why it's vital to have unrealistic goals. I pushed the boundaries with him and challenged his beliefs throughout our coaching. At every session, he was like a sponge, taking on board everything we discussed.

Kai's biggest challenge in the early days was learning to appreciate that his subconscious mind would do just enough to achieve his goal. Becoming a UFC fighter had been his goal and he'd achieved it, and that was reflected in the way he talked about his goals and his identity.

When I asked him what he identified as, he said, 'A UFC fighter.'

I challenged him on that. I said, 'Seriously, mate, the subconscious mind will do just enough, so you'll be in the top eight, the top ten, whatever. You'll be a fighter, but will you be a champion?'

That's when he started to change his goals and his sense of identity. He went from identifying as a UFC fighter to seeing himself as UFC Flyweight Champion.

With Kai, changing his thinking started to build momentum, which reinforced the belief, which reinforced the momentum, which reinforced the belief – and before you know it, he was up there fighting for the title.

His teammates could see the difference in him, not just through his physiology, but also through the language he used. The language UFC Flyweight Champion Kai used was very different to what UFC fighter Kai had used.

For a lot of fighters, their initial goal is to get a contract. Then once they've got that contract, the subconscious goes, 'We've done our job!' That's why it's so important to be specific with language rather than ambiguous. They might get a one-fight or a three-fight contract and their mind will tell them they've achieved their goal and that's enough. Instead, they need to keep pushing with an unrealistic vision to keep themselves on track.

Now, quite a few people have asked me about the fight Kai had against Amir Albazi in June 2023, which ended up with him losing in a controversial split decision. Almost everyone who watched that fight – including most of the media outlets – scored the bout in Kai's favour, but it didn't go that way.

As you get involved in these high-end professional sports, whether you like it or not, there's always going to be a certain level of opinion and politics. Here you've got a young lad who everyone says has been ripped off. The question I'm often asked about that fight is, 'How do you come back from something like that?'

In Kai's case, he will be focusing on the big picture. His energy will be focused on what he can control in order to get back on the ranking in order to get that title fight.

There has to be an intellectual process of going, 'What I can control is where I need to focus. What can I do – both immediately and in the long term – to achieve my goal?'

Let's focus on things that provide a solution.

Chapter 3

YOU CAN'T CHANGE WHAT YOU DON'T FIRST ACKNOWLEDGE

Fear and self-limiting beliefs

What do you really want?

I want to become a performance coach.

I want to run a marathon.

I want to own my own business.

What are some of the limiting beliefs that you have that might be preventing you from doing that?

You know the things that you *can* do. What's important is identifying the things you think you *can't* do, and working out what is stopping you from doing them. Instead of avoiding the things that prevent you from doing something, and settling for a life that is less than the one you want, you have to attack the things that scare you.

Carl Jung is often quoted as saying, 'Where your fear is, there is your task.' That's about understanding your strengths and your weaknesses.

Fear does serve us in some situations – obviously if there's a guy pointing a gun at you, the fear is serving you when it's telling you to get away. Fear is just the subconscious mind doing its job. Sometimes the brain gets it right, and sometimes it doesn't quite. We can't allow fear to override decisions made by the conscious mind.

When fear kicks in, you need to have the ability to decide whether or not whatever's triggering the fear is an immediate threat, and whether you need to go into fight or flight mode and use that adrenaline bump to get away, or whether you should see the fear as a sign that this is something that you probably should be doing, or if it's something that you should investigate more.

There's an acronym that's used to describe fear, which is:

- False
- Evidence
- Appearing
- Real

On the other side of fear, there's a better version of you.

Becoming fearless

I believe we have a responsibility to be the best we can be and to be all we can be. That means overcoming fear and becoming fearless. I think the power of overcoming is one of the biggest gifts we can give ourselves.

When I sat down and was really honest with myself, I identified two things that played no part in my world and which scared the hell out of me: public speaking and academia. Acknowledging and seeking to overcome those fears was a really powerful thing for me.

I had a really significant moment in overcoming my fear. It was in Las Vegas over 30 years ago, where I was given the opportunity to speak in front of 5000 people at the Stardust Hotel. Making it even more intense was the fact that the guest speaker that night was none other than my idol, Jim Rohn. It was an incredible opportunity. I wanted to speak … but I really didn't want to speak. I was so scared that I came up with all these reasons why I shouldn't do it.

It was hot and I was sweating. I turned to Jo and said, 'I can't do it. I'm soaking wet.'

She said, 'Don't worry, I've got another T-shirt.'

After a few more excuses from me, she said, 'Just go! Get out there and do it!'

I did as I was told.

Afterwards, I was sitting in a booth minding my own business and I felt a hand on my shoulder. I turned around – and it was Jim Rohn! He said, 'I was quite impressed with the way you spoke today, young man. You have a bright future ahead of you.'

That was one of the best things that has ever happened to me. The biggest need of an individual is simply to be affirmed and acknowledged, but to be acknowledged by a living legend like Jim Rohn was very significant for me.

Ironically, because I was absolutely not expecting this to happen, I said the dumbest thing I could think of: 'I love you, Jim!'

I felt like an absolute idiot and I could see Jo thinking, 'You just said *what*?'

Now I love being on stage talking, so I can confidently say that I've absolutely conquered that fear.

The last thing for me to conquer was my fear of academia. That scared the shit out of me. I dealt with that fear by saying things like, 'All academics are boring farts.' That was me justifying my position, which was wrong. I did it because we all tend to attack the things we fear.

Eventually, I realised that I had to face my fear, so I signed up to do a degree – and not just any degree, a degree in philosophy and psychology, which meant copious amounts of reading and writing. I didn't decide to do it to help me improve the service I offer my clients. Instead, I'm doing it because I want to prove something to myself.

When it came to completing my first assignment, I had no understanding, no frame of reference and no idea of what I was meant to be doing. I knew I had to do it because it scared me so much. I submitted my first paper online. The question popped up on the screen: 'Are you sure you want to submit this file?'

'NO! I'm not … I don't want to.'

But I hit the button anyway and I got a confirmation that my paper had been submitted. I was so anxious and nervous.

Later, I got an email saying, 'Your paper has been marked.' I got up quietly, walked out to my office and turned on the computer. I opened my email. I clicked the link to take me into the university's site …

I got a B-minus.

I'm a bit of a tough bastard and it's very rare that you'll see me cry, but I burst into tears.

Jo stood at the door and saw me in tears. She was really concerned, so she asked me what had happened. I sobbed and said, 'I got a B-minus!'

She shouted, 'I thought someone had died! We need to celebrate …'

Is that an amazing mark? No, not for a lot of people. But for me, it was life-changing. In the past, all I'd ever got was an F for fail. I'd never achieved anything like this before. I had overcome something that had scared me all my life.

Most people would be terrified at the thought of being expected to pull a truck, get in the boxing ring or bench press a heavy weight. None of that stuff scared me. This, though, was the scariest thing I'd ever done – and I'm proud of myself for stepping up and conquering it.

I'm not intimidated by having to hand in essays now. I've had good ones and bad ones, but I'm working towards fine-tuning the process. After that B-minus, I set myself the goal of getting an A. I'd never had an A in my life, but then I got an A in sociology.

When I started writing, even Grammarly was tapping out! But it's been a really important process to persevere with. I got an essay back with the comment, 'David, I'm really impressed with your writing skills.' I was delighted.

The key thing here being aware of the stories you tell yourself and the limits you impose on yourself. Trying to protect yourself at all times keeps those limits in place. In one English exam at school, I went in, wrote my name on the paper, then left. If you'd told me then that I'd end up writing 250,000 words worth of essays and that I'd get a university degree at the end of it, I'd have been shocked to say the least.

Generally, we are wired to move away from things that we are fearful of. No one wants to go and do something that they don't want to do. An individual may have certain strengths, and that's where they want to stay because they're comfortable there. That feeds the ego beautifully.

Getting out of that comfort zone allows true growth to take place. That means that you have to be prepared to fail. You have to be exposed, and you need to be incredibly honest with yourself.

For me, that looked like saying, 'I'm OK to fail a paper because I know that I'm going to do all that I can to put forward the best possible product that I can. I'm going to take absolute responsibility. I know that if I'm going to do well, I need to study.'

The most incredible project you'll undertake is yourself. There's something beautiful about having the honesty to acknowledge what your fears are and to face up to them, and then to put a plan in place to conquer them.

Self-limiting beliefs

Winning isn't always about coming first. Sometimes it's simply about conquering something that sabotages your potential. For me, a major part of my development was getting to a point of building some confidence and then undertaking that investigation into what some of my limiting beliefs were.

Identifying and deconstructing your self-limiting beliefs will allow you to become fearless. I'm not talking about fearlessness in the sense of picking a fight with someone twice your size, but fearless in the sense that you get out of your own way. Doing that will allow you to fulfil your potential.

The other thing we have to accept is that we will never absolutely fulfil our potential, but it's our responsibility to pursue it and fulfil it as best we can. As the SAS say, 'Who Dares Wins.'

Let's look at what those limiting beliefs are through the lens of feeling really excited about what might happen. Most people refuse to go there because of their ego. Instead, they'll live in denial. But there's nothing more powerful than being honest with yourself, and that's where I want to take my clients. I push, but I'm respectful and strategic in the way I do it.

Give yourself permission

The only way you can really investigate the things that you put in your own way is by giving yourself permission to do it. If you don't give yourself permission, there will still be a certain amount of contamination and filtering that goes on.

Look, it's scary. It's like telling someone to strip off in front of the mirror and inspect every part of their body. But if you don't give yourself that permission, you're not going to recognise when you're getting in your own way.

You need to be fearless without being reckless. You still need to think critically about what you're doing. It's about being intellectual with the process, which means disengaging some of the emotional stuff and seeing it for what it is. Being fearless and reckless is like putting a turbo on a Bambino and heading off down the road at full speed – you're just going to blow the car up!

EXERCISE

Identifying your self-limiting beliefs

You cannot change anything you don't first recognise and acknowledge.

Take a quiet moment somewhere you won't be interrupted. Investigate where your fear lies, then articulate the beliefs that support that fear. The key is to be absolutely honest with yourself.

For example, my fear lay with academia. I had limiting beliefs about my intellect. I had limiting beliefs about my ability to learn. Those limiting beliefs triggered a certain amount of imposter syndrome when I first started coaching.

Where fear lies – that's where I want you to focus, using a lens of being curious about it. From there, you can develop strategies to become fearless and work to change those beliefs.

> Once you've acknowledged the limitation, tell yourself, 'I'm going to conquer this.' This is the importance of becoming, of moving away and moving towards. As you work through these things, you overcome, and therefore become a better version of yourself.

With that process in place, you start building this momentum that allows you to start overcoming those limiting beliefs through being more conscious and taking action. You go through a paradigm change. Suddenly, all these limiting beliefs disappear.

I've had eureka moments with my clients, where I can see them realise what they've been doing to get in their own way. Sometimes that can involve sitting down and having those conversations with someone like myself, or just having meaningful conversations with yourself.

For me, the limiting belief was based on my experience failing everything at school. I could go and pull a 28-tonne truck, but the thought of writing an essay filled me with fear.

When it comes to facing those fears, sometimes you'll need to be realistic in the timing. Even though it's appropriate to challenge your self-limiting beliefs, you have to take a grounded approach to it.

In my experience with academia, I needed to have the time to focus. That first essay I submitted, I'd never been so anxious about anything. I knew it was the first of many, and I had no idea how it was going to go. Getting that B-minus was really special because I felt like I'd won. From there, I built momentum.

Experience and hard work will condition your body and brain to overcome self-limiting beliefs. Think about those surfers you see on those 30-foot waves. Most people – including me – look at them and think, 'Are you serious?!'

Most of them have been surfing since they were kids, they've been bashed around by the waves and they didn't die, so they continue doing something that they've become passionate about. Once you find that passion, it will take you far.

Mind your language

One of the key things I say to my clients is 'mind your language'. Many people are outcome orientated, and that can include having a focus on negative outcomes. Their attitude towards the outcome is reflected in the language they use.

I was a prime example of that. I used to call myself a dumbarse all the time. You've got to be your own best friend – you wouldn't say that about your best friend, so don't put yourself down like that. If we talk to ourselves and about ourselves with this kind of language, we're giving ourselves permission to self-sabotage.

When I started changing my language and took responsibility for what I was saying, that all changed.

Most people are aware of their negative self-talk, but they just surrender to it, so that it becomes habitual. You cannot change anything you do not first acknowledge. You've got to wake up to it.

Perception is projection. What we verbalise becomes our reality. When I hear words of possibility, opportunity and gratitude, as opposed to words of doom, gloom and frustration, I know things have really changed for that person. When we mind our language, we're able to become more assertive and we can move away from excuses.

I had one client who had a particular self-limiting belief. He had an issue with any short putts that he had to take, say from 12 feet. Those are the ones that a lot of people think are easy, but they're not. (His 12-foot putt can be replaced with any self-limiting belief you might have.)

I told him that he had to mind his language when he was framing his representation of that putt. 'The brain is predictive, so if you're constantly affirming what you don't want to happen – "I always stuff up these short putts" – then the probability of that action being repeated and reinforced is increased.'

Develop a new narrative

Under stress, we tend to go back to what we do naturally. Instead of letting this happen, we want to create a new narrative or belief system, because what we had in the past was dysfunctional. We want to develop better coping mechanisms moving forward.

You might regress back to telling your victim story because, unconsciously, that's what your habit is. I'll stop you and say, 'In the past.'

If you try to justify your victim story, I'll stop you again and ask, 'In what way does the continuous representation and verbalisation of that problem really serve you?'

EXERCISE

Change the CD

The analogy I use is that our language is a bit like a CD.

Imagine you and I are going on a road trip. What's some music you absolutely hate, that will drive you nuts? Imagine that's my favourite album, so I put it on. I know all the words so I'm singing along with it.

Now imagine yourself as that CD. All you're doing is constantly playing yourself these dysfunctional tracks. I want you to interrupt yourself, scratch that old CD (that you hate) and lay down new tracks.

When you start doing that, you become aware of it. Then you'll be able to catch yourself when that old CD starts up.

If you need help with catching yourself and holding yourself accountable, maybe ask what some of my clients ask themselves: 'What would Big Dave say?'

I'd say, 'In the past.'

Framing the belief

Perception becomes your projection, so you need to be consciously aware of what you are telling yourself. The brain is predictive. When you're constantly talking about how bad you are, how hard things are, your brain will go out of its way to find and show you evidence of whatever you're telling it. When you start to change your framing and your perception of the world, words start to change from necessity and survival to opportunity and possibility – and that's beautiful, because change can then really start to take place.

You have to change the way you frame your beliefs. You cannot change anything you don't first recognise, so you've got to recognise that framing in and of itself is limiting your ability to progress.

Sometimes when people are asked to face up to their self-limiting belief, their response is to say, 'Well, it's just the reality. There's evidence for it, you know!' I get that there might be evidence for what they believe – because they *have* been messing up 12-foot putts – but holding on to that belief doesn't help anyone move forward.

In those situations, I start with some affirmations. Try saying, 'Twelve-foot putts are easy for me,' and, 'I'm always confident over a twelve-foot putt.'

Affirmations

We have busy lives. A lot of people have great intentions to take time for being mindful. Often, though, they just don't make the time. When we talk about mindfulness, some people like to meditate, some people do yoga and others actively visualise, but those activities aren't for everyone.

What I care about is getting results. Creating affirmations can prepare the subconscious mind. They take very little time out of your day but are very powerful.

When constructing affirmations, it's important that each one is powerful and assertive, and it needs to be in the present tense – so 'I am' not 'I will be'. That's vital, because the subconscious mind has no concept of reality or time. It only knows now.

A lot of people will have an affirmation that goes something like, 'I want to be the best I can.'

The subconscious mind doesn't recognise the future, 'I want *to be*'. Instead, putting that affirmation into the present tense, it should say, 'I *am* the best version of myself.'

'I am, right now ...' is an important part of how you construct any affirmation. Using present tense is important because performance is in the now.

When you look at the construction of an argument, there will often be two premises that support a conclusion. One premise supporting a conclusion is not as convincing as two. The same goes for affirmations.

The first affirmation I recommend to all my clients is:

I, [full name], am undoubtedly proud of myself.

My first coach, Clive Litten, who was a massive influence on me, was the master of coming up with the most elegant affirmations. They were almost like poetry. He is the one who helped me to set that affirmation. 'Undoubtedly' is a really key word, because you never want to doubt your ability or doubt your own pride in yourself.

This is our foundational affirmation, which is universal to everyone. It doesn't matter what the situation is; this affirmation is flexible and will help to build the pillars of confidence.

A second foundational affirmation I use is:

I give myself permission to be world class.

I used the word 'permission' a lot because it's incredibly important. It tells your brain that it's allowed to act as if it's world class.

The third affirmation should focus on the specific situation related to your goal. For example, when taking 12-foot putts, speaking in front of large groups, or going into a title fight.

A client talked to me about their self-limiting belief around speaking in front of authority figures. As part of his work, this client was expected to speak in front of the prime minister and various government ministers, and the thought of it freaked him out. For him, his third affirmation was:

Everyone loves what I have to say.

This affirmation has to be a representation of the outcome. For a swimmer who gets anxious on race day, their affirmation might be something like:

The more I swim, the more confident I become. Race day is easy for me.

My three affirmations are:

I, David Paul Niethe, am undoubtedly proud of myself.
Every time I open my mouth, I get new business.
Everyone loves what I have to say.

EXERCISE

Creating affirmations

Most clients I speak to identify that they're lacking in one of two key resources: confidence and energy.

Don't think too hard about your answers here.

- Of the two, which is more important for you right now?
- When thinking about being incredibly confident, what colour is confidence for you?
- When thinking about being really energetic, what colour is energy for you?

Which colour you choose doesn't matter – it just has to have some meaning to you. If your answer was yellow, then use yellow text on a black background and type this out:

'I, [full name], am undoubtedly proud of myself.'

The colour yellow will subconsciously trigger feelings of confidence. That trigger colour will improve the probability of eliciting in you a state of confidence (or energy, or whatever resource you require).

Print off your affirmations in your chosen colour, and put them everywhere you'll see them regularly.

These affirmations are a form of subconscious programming. We can use this process to help programme our minds to reframe our beliefs. I have a client who has his affirmations printed out and posted on his wardrobe door. Sometimes when he opens his wardrobe he'll be aware of them hanging there, and sometimes he won't notice them. Whether he registers them consciously or not doesn't matter, because they're constantly there, programming his brain.

I've had people laminate these affirmations and stick them in the shower, or on the wall behind the toilet. They don't need to be in obvious places, just somewhere you're going to see them regularly. You want to be constantly programming your brain. Three or four months later, there'll be a change in your language, behaviour and perception.

Initially, when you hang them up, you'll be aware of your affirmations: 'I open my wardrobe and there it is hanging there.' But over a period of time, they'll 'disappear' and you won't even notice that they're there. Even though you're not noticing their presence, their effect remains.

It's almost like you're giving yourself evidence in a process of convincing your brain to accept a new narrative. We've got these affirmations with an associated belief. Then we've got our specific affirmation, and we're constantly providing evidence that reinforces that, so the brain goes, 'The negative programme is not working. I'll have to replace it.'

That's proven in neurology – new connections and neural pathways are being created all the time. You're reprogramming your brain into the winning mindset.

Representation and framing

Another thing to consider, along with subconscious reprogramming, is *conscious* awareness of representation and framing. The best way to summarise that is to think about winter. In winter, some people bitch and moan about the cold. Other people happily ski. It's all about how you frame it.

When you start to become aware of the limitations you're creating through verbalisation and internal representation, and when you think about your goals and the ways you're not quite congruent with them, that's where you can start to become more self-supportive.

Understand that on this journey, you're going to fuck up and fail, but you can reframe your perception of failure. When they hear the word 'failure', a lot of people have an internal feeling that is very much linked to shame or embarrassment.

It's easy to say, 'You've got to reframe failure', but in order to do that you need to understand the importance of failure, and to understand failure you need to build a stronger self-image.

When you haven't got a very strong self-image, each time you fail it's going to reinforce the pattern of dysfunction or your low sense of self-esteem. When you have a strong self-image, you've got a foundation from which you can navigate through failure while not being vulnerable to shame, embarrassment or whatever other negative feelings you might attach to the concept.

As you learn to reframe things and manage your perceptions and talk, you build more and more resilience, which ultimately takes you to a place where you become free. For me, that's a place where I don't care what other people think – and in that place, I am free of all the negative feelings attached to the concept of failure.

PROFILE

Affirmations and overcoming

Michael Hendry

Professional golfer

- Turned professional in 2005
- 16 professional wins at time of writing
- Indonesia Open winner 2010
- New Zealand PGA Championship winner 2012, 2013

- Japan Golf Tour winner 2015
- New Zealand Open winner 2017
- Victoria Open winner 2023
- Clearwater Open winner 2023

When I first met Michael, he had a multitude of things he wanted to achieve in his golfing career. Together, we looked over these goals then became laser-focused on the events he had coming up.

As he is very visual, we decided to create a vision board, which included a cheque to represent his goal of being able to earn a living from playing golf. He achieved that goal when he turned professional in 2005. Since then, he's become one of New Zealand's most successful golfers.

After we'd created a set of affirmations to support these goals, he was so committed to them that he got one set of them laminated and put them in the shower. That's a great idea, because when you're having a shower it's time for yourself and there are no distractions. That can stimulate you to then start the visualisation process.

I've been working with Michael for more than 20 years. Progressively, as with a lot of clients, I've worked less and less with him as he's become clearer on his goals. I'm always there if they need me, though.

In May 2023, he announced that he'd been diagnosed with leukaemia. In order to undertake treatment, he took leave from his golf career, which meant missing out on competing in the British Open – for which he'd qualified – in July of that same year.

In his announcement, he wrote, 'This is the fight of my life, a fight for my life, but one I am determined to win.'

The first session I had with him after his diagnosis was emotional and uplifting at the same time. When I was talking to Mike, he said, 'I just want to get back into golf.' I could hear his passion for the game in his voice.

I said, 'Mike, you and I are going to sit down and we're going to start creating one of the greatest stories in golf comeback history.' You should have seen the look on his face – it was like, 'Yes! I'm back.' That's what people love – sometimes, it's just about someone having that belief in them.

He is one determined man. We had some quite open conversations about dying and death, and he's always appreciated the fact that I'm consistently open and honest with him. That's about the trust factor between client and coach.

A mere four months after his diagnosis, he was back playing professional golf on New Zealand's Charles Tour. That greatest comeback in golfing history came about at just his second tournament back in the game: in October 2023, he won the Clearwater Open. It also happened to be his 44th birthday. That win made gave him his ninth title on the Charles Tour, making him the tour's most successful player ever.

Chapter 4

PROTECT YOURSELF AT ALL TIMES

Building a strong self-image

Most people fall when they get to the first hurdle. This happens because they're so weak in their mindset, so averse to failure and so concerned with what other people think that they've developed a weak self-image. That results in them making the mistake of settling for a life that is less than the one they deserve.

The people who have – or are well on the way to having – a winning mindset know that there is no such thing as failure. There is only learning, and if you're learning, you're moving forward. Remember that fear is:

- False
- Evidence
- Appearing
- Real

Once you're able to reframe the things you fear, you need to then start to strengthen and protect your self-image. Self-image is what you think about yourself and the beliefs you have about yourself. When you have a strong self-image it supports your journey towards creating what you want.

Self-image is like a crystal-clear bowl

Think of your self-image as a crystal-clear bowl full of crystal-clear water. Within it lie your visions and your goals; when it's crystal clear, you can see where you're going.

Self-awareness is the key here. Studies have shown that, on average, we all have between 60,000 and 80,000 thoughts a day. Each and every one of those thoughts has the power to either contribute or contaminate.

Imagine those 60,000 to 80,000 thoughts. If we have a whole lot of them that are negative and we're not consciously aware of it, each one adds a small amount of dye to that crystal-clear water. Initially, each negative thought and each small amount of dye will seem insignificant, but if you have 20,000 of them, that stains the whole bowl and you lose sight of who you are and where you're going. You lose sight of your vision and your goals.

A lot of people get into the habit of having negative thoughts about themselves when they're still very young. When young people are bullied, they often respond by either having negative thoughts about themselves because other people do, or they might become the class clown and try to make people laugh – often at their own expense – which lessens the chance of them being bullied.

One of the most profound things I've ever heard comes from boxing, and that is the last thing the referee says to two fighters before they come out banging: 'Protect yourself at all times.'

When you build a strong self-image and you become conscious of it, you then learn to protect yourself. There's something really powerful in that.

We can protect our self-image through our consciousness and our self-awareness. The basic principle here is that you cannot change anything you don't first acknowledge – this is why we have to be consciously aware. Underlying that is remembering to 'mind your language', because your language becomes your map of the world.

When you have that self-awareness, you can capture yourself before your thinking becomes detrimental. You can navigate away from thinking, doing or saying things that won't serve you.

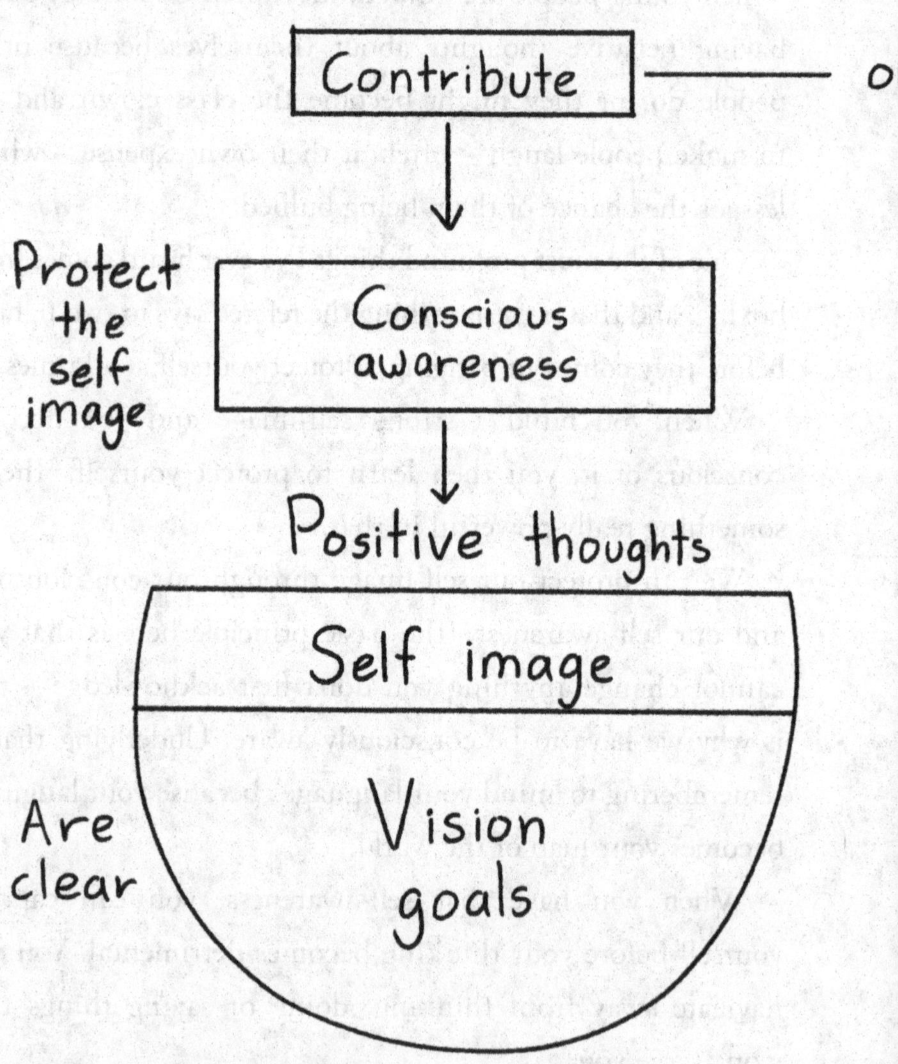
60,000–80,000
thoughts a day either
Contribute
or
Protect
the
self
image
Conscious
awareness
Positive thoughts
Self image
Are
clear
Vision
goals

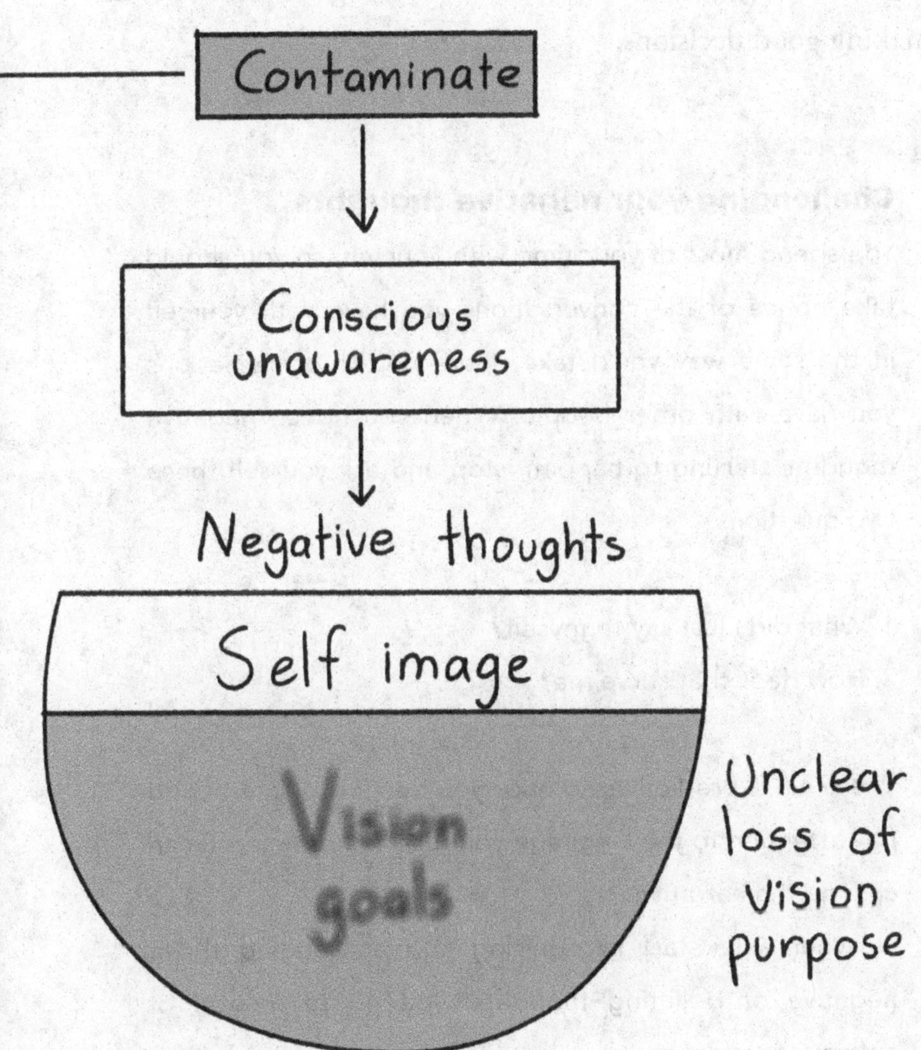
Contaminate
Conscious unawareness
Negative thoughts
Self image
Vision goals
Unclear loss of vision purpose

What psychological and physiological state do we have to be in to make good decisions? We need to be calm. If you are constantly calm and not reactionary, that allows you to be more effective with your thinking, which will result in you making good decisions. Ultimately, a good life is about making good decisions.

EXERCISE

Challenging your negative thoughts

You spend most of your time with yourself, so you should take notice of the conversations you have with yourself in the same way you'd take notice of the conversations you have with other people. When you notice negative thoughts starting to happen, stop and ask yourself these two questions:

1. What did I just say to myself?
2. How does that serve me?

The brain is predictive, so once you become aware of and pay attention to the language your brain chooses, you can change the narrative.

When you start recognising and challenging those negative or polluting thoughts, you go to a level of awareness where you start becoming more self-supportive.

When you start becoming more self-supportive, you open the gateway for the most beautiful thing: momentum. Your self-image strengthens and you start to grow in a positive way.

Minimising negative thoughts

I want people to realise the importance of minimising negative thoughts, rather than maximising positive thoughts. If you build your whole existence on the sand of relentless positivity, a lot of people will fall through the cracks very quickly.

We've got to appreciate that, to a certain point, we are going to have negative thoughts. Even then, they serve us in the sense that they help us to understand, recognise and acknowledge our positive thoughts and our happiness.

It's not ideal to be in a negative state. If we minimise the negative thoughts, it doesn't necessarily mean that we're happy, but we're functional.

You're not always going to be happy and thinking positive thoughts. However, ideally, we want the compass to point more in the direction of happiness than away from it.

EXERCISE

BED and OAR

An easy way to think about the thoughts you have and the words you use is to remind yourself of OAR and BED. It looks like this:

O wnership
A ccountability 5% – top performers
R esponsibility

B lame
E xcuse 95% – live below the line
D enial

Most people operate from below the line, in a place of blame, excuse and denial. I want people to operate from above the line and take ownership, accountability and responsibility for their thoughts, words and actions.

When you catch yourself getting into that negative thought pattern, ask yourself, 'Does this help me to get out of BED?'

Your state is a choice

You have to appreciate that your state is a choice. What that basically means is we don't disengage the feelings and the learnings, but we take them for what they are and we learn to reframe them in a way that serves us.

When I tell people that their state is a choice, I often hear, 'That's bullshit! I should be allowed to feel what I feel!'

To them I say, yes, to a certain point. But you've got to be very careful with that because it can easily lead you to a point where, if you don't interrupt it, you will constantly feel sad. Does that serve you?

People are good at creating their victim story, and by doing that, they limit themselves. We're thrown into this world. We don't get to choose when we arrive or who our parents are. Whether we like it or not, we are here, and I believe that we have a responsibility to be the best we can be.

Most people react. I need you to respond. Filter information with a clear intention of it leading towards a solution, as opposed to feeding the negativity and manifesting more stress and dysfunction.

I'm not suggesting that you should never feel sad. Of course, when something bad happens – like when someone dies – you have to take the time to process that. But to hold onto that sadness forever will not serve you. Those negative feelings can start to fester. In protecting yourself, have that conscious awareness to say, 'How do I reframe this to serve me?'

A prime example of this is Viktor Frankl. Now there's a man who had the ability to reframe something to give it some sense of meaning that could serve him.

An Austrian Jewish psychologist, Frankl had been married just nine months when he and his family were sent to Theresienstadt concentration camp in 1942. Over the next three years, he spent time in four different camps. His mother and brother were both murdered in gas chambers and his father and wife both died of preventable diseases.

After the war, Frankl wrote *Man's Search for Meaning* about his experiences in those camps. While the book detailed his horrific experiences throughout his time as a prisoner, its main focus was on what gave him the will to survive. He wrote that he wanted to 'convey to the reader by way of concrete example that life holds a potential meaning under any conditions, even the most miserable ones.'

Imagine if everyone had the ability to use their hardships and difficulties to create some meaning in their lives instead of creating a victim story.

The disappointments in our lives sometimes become the biggest blessings if we learn to reframe them. They can be something that ignites passion in us to overcome and do great things.

As in example, you often hear about people being made redundant and, by necessity, having to adapt, take risks and try new things. While losing their job might have felt scary and difficult, they are then able to reframe it as an opportunity to create a new career for themselves. They could have taken that jump earlier, but they didn't because they were comfortable. There was no need to make change. Yet that's the time when you need to start some conversations about what you want out of life.

Going back to Frankl, he said, paraphrasing Goethe: 'If we take a man as he really is, we make him worse. But if we overestimate him … we promote him to what he really can be.'[2]

Having high expectations of someone (including yourself) can ignite something within for them to become better than they currently are. In some ways, that's what I do. I take someone who wants more from life and allow them to understand and manifest a better possible version of themselves.

Feeling stuck

I generally deal with clients who are really motivated to get the best out of themselves. However, if you're feeling stuck and not sure how to move forward, here's my advice:

> *The quality of your life is directly related to the quality of the questions you ask yourself and others.*

If you're feeling stuck and don't know what you should be doing, ask yourself a better question. Asking yourself, 'Why am I so unhappy?' doesn't serve you. Instead, ask yourself,

'What are two things I can think of right now that will make me happy?'

If you're going to unblock, you need to challenge yourself to ask those better-quality questions.

When working on those questions, remember to mind your language. If you repeatedly tell yourself something is hard, your brain will learn to perceive it as such. If you catch yourself saying, 'It's hard for me to think positively when I'm feeling like this', your brain will make it so. Instead, think about how you can reframe that to serve you.

You'll always put barriers in your own way, because humans are very good at being stubborn. All that language of 'It's so hard' and 'I can't because …' just supports your victim story. You've put in a lot of work to get to where you are in that victim state, and if you really want to break free, you're going to have to do the work to get out of it. Why? Because being miserable doesn't serve you.

If you don't feel that you can turn it around yourself, seek external help. Find the kind of help you need, whether that's from family, friends, your doctor or a counsellor.

Protect yourself at all times

Language

Part of learning to protect yourself at all times is constantly being mindful of how you are representing your model of the world, both verbally and through your behaviour. If you are consciously aware of using words of opportunity and possibility, that puts you on a path in a wonderful way. Others will be working on language that reinforces their victim story. Language is powerful, so the language you use should match your values.

In my work world, a lot of my language is definitely male-orientated in the sense that, when we're talking about high performance, it is towards the concept of a warrior. However, there are times when I have to be very careful and selective with my language because there's going to be a certain level of sensitivity and I want to respect that. Using the appropriate words is not a sign of weakness at all, because the measure of all communication is in the response. If I get the right response, I can build on that.

I've had women with low self-esteem come to see me. They have talent, but they constantly self-sabotage. With them, I've chosen to use softer language initially before building it up. This is where it's important for me to read the situation closely and to understand just how far I can push them in order to get the necessary breakthroughs.

Over a couple of years of working together, I'll notice a change in the way that they represent themselves and verbalise. A couple of them have kept diaries and I've encouraged them to go back over those to really understand the distinct change that has occurred in the language that they use. Ultimately, that helps set them free.

The people around you

The people around you can have a huge impact on your self-image – if you let them. When you have a strong self-image, you're less likely to fold to the will of the collective.

To achieve our goals, we need to learn to put our own needs first. A lot of people are highly agreeable and won't put themselves first – by doing that, they're giving their power away.

EXERCISE

Putting yourself first

Right now, I want you to stop what you're doing and say, 'I give myself permission to put myself first.'

Repeat this as often as you need to, until it becomes anchored in your subconscious and your behaviours begin to reflect it.

People are like your thoughts – there are two types: those that contribute and those that contaminate.

There's a saying that there are people you meet for a reason, a season or a lifetime. It's OK to let people go, and it's OK for people not to stay in your life. If you find that you have people in your life who serve only to contaminate your clarity, challenge your values and distract you from your goals, move on from them. This could be that mate who always tells you to ditch training to go to the pub, or someone who constantly laughs or rolls their eyes when you talk about the goals you've set for yourself. Letting go of these people can be a really challenging process, but you'll be much happier on the other side of it.

Remember: how you represent, create and frame your world is represented by your language. Your intention is to be clear about what you want, but your attention is compromised. That's sometimes reflected in your language. You might hear yourself saying things like, 'It's hard to let people go…'

You've got to be careful of the language you use when you realise that's what you need to do. If you constantly repeat to yourself that letting these people go is difficult, it will give you elbow room to make excuses and not do it.

That said, you will find it easy to let some people go because it will be clear that they are not adding anything to your life.

It's also important that we acknowledge when someone is potentially contaminating our lives. We need to have the courage to speak up or take action in these situations, knowing that some relationships will need to be reframed because of their depth or length.

It's essential to understand that we teach people how to treat us. If you have a family member or friend who is constantly pulling you down, you need to have the resilience within and the belief in your vision to say, 'Don't talk to me like that' or 'Don't treat me like that.'

It's important to become self-aware and selective, because you are going to meet people who will want to steal your energy. Not all of your friends are your friends. You'll meet people who, when you have success, will say, 'I'm so happy for you', but you know that, inside, they're envious or being judgemental. They never think about the fact you've worked your arse off to earn what you've achieved.

There'll be people who say things like, 'You're so lucky you got that job', or promotion, or house, or holiday. Clive taught me that the best response to comments like that is simply: 'Yes.'

That said, one of your biggest sources of confidence is your support network. Powerful stuff can happen when you've got a good support network around you.

There's a spectrum we're all on in terms of our need for connection. I'm highly extroverted, so I need a lot of connection. I'm very lucky that I can connect with people through my work. I've created my environment so I'm surrounded by people I love, and I see a lot of people who are of interest to me. When I go out, I spend time with like-minded people. By doing that, I'm protecting myself at all times by spending my time with people whose company I find fulfilling.

I'm also very selective about who I listen to and who I hang out with. I've got mates that I talk to maybe only three or four times a year, but I've been mates with them for decades. Yes, I've had friends come and go, but I'm very lucky to have had that core group of friends. I know they've got my back because when I've been in tough times, they've been there for me. It's only through those real tough times that your true, genuine friends will show themselves.

When you think about your vision, you can be sure that your true friends will be there to support it, undeniably.

These friendships are a bit like a video game. You might hit pause and not speak to each other for a while, but when you hit play again the timeframe is irrelevant. It's amazing. We don't need to communicate all the time because none of us needs that constant reassurance. We know we can rely on each other no matter what because true friends will always support you when you need it.

The power of putting yourself first

People often come up to have a chat with me at events. I'm always blown away when they tell me that they've heard me speak before and that it prompted them to change their lives. There have been times when I've ended up in tears as I've listened to their stories of overcoming huge obstacles in order to put themselves first and make meaningful change.

I've heard stories of people enduring domestic abuse and gang violence, overcoming alcohol and drug addiction, and walking away from everything they've known in order to build better lives for themselves.

One woman told me she hadn't wanted to come to my talk, but her friend had dragged her along. She said that what had really stuck with her was me saying that people had to get clear on their vision and commit to it with conviction. With that in mind, she said she'd started to value herself, and she gave herself permission to be selfish, to put herself first. From that moment on, she'd worked hard on changing herself, which then allowed her to help make changes in the lives of people around her.

Coaches and mentors

When it comes to building strong self-image, one of the most powerful resources you can have is a good mentor or coach. My first-ever coach, Clive, taught me and held me to account, and I love him for that. He was very hard on me, to a point. He would never have sat there and said to me, 'Oh, you poor thing! Are you feeling OK? How do you feel about that?'

I always showed up for my appointment on time, if not early. If he asked me to write something, I wrote it. That came down to respect.

We need to seek out mentors who are willing to tell us the truth when we need to pull our heads in, when we're making excuses for ourselves and when we're falling back into our victim stories.

What other people think

Freedom is not giving a toss what other people think of you. When you get to that point, you will come across people who are envious of you and the life you've created. That's on them. I tell clients, 'I never, ever want you to put anyone on a pedestal – including yourself.' I also tell them that what other people think of them is none of their business.

We can go to the extreme and think that we're better than other people (and we've got the Instagram to prove it!). If you need to feel that you're better than other people, that's not about living your core values or having strong self-image.

There's something really nice in not caring what other people think. You can be at peace. When you're in that place of being undoubtedly proud of yourself and what you've created, you will attract people who really respect what you've achieved.

When you truly are in that zone, you don't give a fuck if other people give a fuck. It's a wonderful place to be, and from there, I've created some really beautiful, genuine friendships. I've also found that I'm comfortable with myself.

Be curious

Curiosity combined with a vision, combined with minimising contaminating thoughts and building belief systems that are supportive – what a wonderful way to navigate through life.

Despite being diagnosed with dyslexia, I've fallen in love with books. It's curiosity; when you stay curious it keeps those neural pathways opening up and your mental flexibility keeps stretching. I believe it's important for everyone to have a curious mind, because that way you are always seeking and you will not dwell on things.

Having a high level of curiosity is a wonderful asset for navigating through life. There's real power in living life through the lens of wonder. When you see life as something to be curious about, you're always going to be investigating and enjoying it.

The opposite to being curious is to think of life as boring and approach it with fear. Curiosity allows you to override any sort of fear, because you know that out there on the other side of it is where possibilities lie.

Most people frame things to subdue, limit or control. Always reframe things to serve you. When you're reframing your perception of something, if you see it through the lens of being curious it can reduce your emotional response. 'Oh, right, that's really interesting. I can see why I thought that …' Curiosity provides a far better foundation to investigate from than a place of being overwhelmed with emotion – be that anger, sadness, hurt, frustration … whatever.

Being constantly curious can help you deal with some of the challenges of life. Instead of worrying about the future, try approaching it with a sense of curiosity.

This reminds me of what I call 'Christmas Eve syndrome': that feeling you had when you knew Santa was coming and you knew you were going to get something, but you didn't know what it was going to be. You were just excited about the fact that you were going to get something. That's the place where I want to be. I want to always have that sense of excitement and curiosity. What a beautiful way to live life – it's like being a child.

Remember Nietzsche's ideas about the transition from the camel to the lion and the lion to the child? I interpret a child as someone who is fearless, curious and energised. Think about what it's like looking after a toddler. It's full on! They don't comprehend danger, and there's something wonderful in their enthusiasm. Learning to approach life with that same level of fearlessness, curiosity and energy is all part of developing the winning mindset and will really help you to achieve your goals.

Protect the collective

Every team – whether sporting or business – is made up of individuals, each of whom has 60,000 to 80,000 thoughts a day. Those thoughts all have the potential to support or contaminate not only their own vision and goals, but also those of the rest of their team.

Those team members not only have to protect themselves at all times but also the rest of the collective. To do this, they need to take individual responsibility for working towards a clear team vision and a common set of goals. They need to bring the right mindset to a team environment by taking personal responsibility and being consciously aware of anything that might contaminate the team image.

The one goal that I guarantee every team will have is that they are there to win. If someone consistently brings contaminating thoughts or actions to that team, their ability to win will be compromised. It doesn't matter how hard everyone else works, that contamination can spoil the team's efforts.

To deal with someone who might be contaminating your team's efforts, the first step is to identify what is happening. The next step is to have an honest, open conversation with them. It's possible that they're going through a tough time; if that's the case, encourage them to get the help they need. However, if their attitude is that everything sucks, or everything's an issue but none of it is their responsibility, you need to put in place the necessary steps for them to exit the team or they will continue to contaminate.

Chapter 5

WE TEACH PEOPLE HOW TO TREAT US

Consistency, accountability and gratitude

We but mirror the world. All the tendencies present in the outer world are to be found in the world of our body. If we could change ourselves, the tendencies in the world would also change. As a man changes his own nature, so does the attitude of the world change towards him. This is the divine mystery supreme. A wonderful thing it is and the source of our happiness. We need not wait to see what others do.

—Mahatma Gandhi, *Indian Opinion*, 1913

We all know people who come through with the same problem time and time again, and you just sit there thinking,

I've already heard this and told you what I think. What I get upset with is how people are very quick to say that they're unhappy, but that statement is not matched with behaviours aimed at making change.

I believe that, at the end of the day, if it's going to be, it's up to me. If you really want to make a difference, first start on yourself. If people focused on reality and what they can change for the better, what sort of world would it be?

It's easy to get overwhelmed by everything that's happening in the world. If everyone was working on themselves in an active, conscious way, in a way where they make themselves their personal project, and in a way where they treat others with respect, the world would be a much better place.

The majority of your focus should be in support of the self. As an existentialist, I believe that we're thrown into this world and it's our responsibility to become the best version of ourselves.

In order for something to change, something has to change. That change can be something small, but when it's done with consistency it can lead to much bigger things. What is the key to consistency? The key to consistency is consistency. With consistency comes momentum, and momentum is one of the most powerful forces there is.

How do you get better at something? Through practice and absolute conviction.

Challenge yourself to change

US Navy Admiral William McRaven put it best when he said, 'If you want to change the world, start off by making your bed.' (And remember, in order to make your bed, you have to get out of BED!)

To that I'd add: Before you worry about anyone else, make your own bed. Think about the immediate – yourself. Once you've tidied up you, by all means start on other people. But who among us has got their shit completely together? Not many people.

Make good choices

A couple of key elements of the winning mindset are tenacity – you need to have a tenacious resolve – and selfishness. Most people think being self-interested is a bad thing, but you have to be selfish if you're going to achieve real greatness. I'm not saying you need to become self-centred and nasty, but what I am saying is that you have to be clear on your priorities in life in relation to the goals you've set.

Friends might say, 'Hey, we're going to a party. Are you coming?' You know you've got a comp coming up; you have to do the right thing for yourself and for your long-term goals. It's about being self-aware and being clear on what you want for yourself above everything else.

We're supposed to be so altruistic that focusing on what we want or what's good for us as an individual is seen as negative. I'm not dismissing altruism at all, but if you want to be, say, a world champion, or you want to achieve a huge goal, especially as an individual outside a team setting, it's *you* stepping in the ring – not your mates and not your colleagues. You may have a few key support people, but no one else is going to have the same passion about achieving your goal as you do.

A lot of people talk about the authentic self and mindfulness. I talk about being self-aware. Regardless of whether you call it mindfulness or self-awareness, these concepts certainly have power to help you take charge of your mindset when you care for them appropriately.

A great affirmation is: 'I make good choices.' It's so versatile. So many times I've laid that out as an affirmation for clients, and they've come back and told me about times when they've made good choices.

Make your expectations clear

We teach people how to treat us. I'm a massive fan of that idea. If you make your expectations of people clear from the outset, it minimises the chance of misunderstandings. By telling people what you expect from them and being clear about what you expect of yourself, you're teaching them – and yourself – how to treat you.

A client will show up and I'll say, 'You want to get value out of today?'

'Yes.'

'Then where's your book and your pen? Did I make it clear to you that I don't write reports? Everything that is recorded goes in *your* book. So you can sit here and nod your head and think we're having a really good conversation, but what have you documented from that conversation?'

I'll hold them to account. I can be a stubborn old prick at times, but I get results and I pride myself on that. I'm not interested in blowing smoke up anyone's arse. I'm interested in getting the very best out of people. That's my passion.

Now I'm very clear with new clients about what I expect from them, before our first meeting. I'll tell them that I expect them to arrive early and be ready and waiting to begin on time.

We teach people how to treat us. If I don't value my time, how can I expect other people to?

That was something that Clive taught me as well. You showed up on time and you were prepared. I think he was harder on me than most, but in hindsight, I think it was because he truly believed in me, loved me and knew I was capable of a lot more. He saw my potential even when I didn't see it – and sometimes that's what a good coach does. A coach can sometimes see what you can't.

I can say something to a client that, even though they don't believe it, will become embedded in their brain, and over a period of time it will then be reflected in their performance, their language, their representation and their framing.

Guard your time

One thing I can't stand is people saying, 'I'm so bored.' Are you serious? Bored? There's not enough time for that!

When I talk about freedom, the most important thing for me is not money, it's time – and I don't want to waste it. I am very good at managing my time. That is the most important resource we all have, and that's why I like to organise my weeks. I want to ensure that by the end of the week I've got everything I possibly can out of my time.

The only way to manage time is to become time aware. What does that mean? Let's look at an example. If an organisation asks me to come and speak to their team, I'll let them know that I expect them to be ready for me to start at the agreed time.

When the day of the talk comes, irrespective of whether people are still dribbling into the venue, I'll start at the time we've agreed. That way, the onus is on the people attending to be there on time.

If you're a golfer and you miss a tee time, you're disqualified. In the world of high-performance sport, I need athletes to be absolutely aware of time and know how to manage their time.

If they're going to be true high-performers, good management of time is a prerequisite.

The biggest resource for me is my time. It is not to be wasted, and I will not allow people to rip me off and steal it. That's not to say I don't ever switch off. There is a time to be timely and a time to chill out. That balance is important.

Time is so important to me because for a large portion of my life I lived by other people's timetables. I still have an alarm clock next to my bed. It sits there as a reminder to me to appreciate what I've created – and it occasionally comes in handy when I have an early flight to catch.

It reminds me of Epicurus, who said, 'He who is not satisfied with a little is satisfied with nothing.'

Epicurus went to great lengths to appreciate simple things. He loved cheese, but largely lived on bread and water. That way, when he was brought a small pot of cheese, he saw it as something indulgent that he would look forward to and enjoy. Similarly, even after 30 years, not having to set an alarm to get me out of bed in the morning feels indulgent to me.

EXERCISE

Prioritising your tasks

Set aside 15 minutes every morning to prioritise your tasks for the day, using the Rocks Pebbles Sand time-management method.

Imagine your day as a jar. In it, you must fit all the things you want to get done that day. First in go the rocks, which take up most of the space. Around them will fit some smaller pebbles. Once the jar looks pretty full, that's when the sand goes in to fill up the small spaces between the rocks and the pebbles.

The rocks are the things that will take up most of your time, but which are non-negotiable in order for you to achieve your goals. Usually, there'll be fewer than five of these.

The pebbles are the smaller things you need to do, which don't have such a strict deadline. These will take up less time but that are still important.

The sand is made up of daily tasks that can be done quickly, but it's not such a big deal if they don't get done.

Write a list of all your tasks for the day.

Once you've completed the list, decide whether each item on it is a rock, a pebble or sand.

Prioritising your tasks in this way will give you a clear picture of how you need to divide your time for the day and where your focus should be.

Stop apologising

When I tell people I don't want their apologies, they're usually quite shocked. Then I go on to explain. I say something like, 'I think it's great that you have the respect to apologise, but you shouldn't put yourself in the position of needing to apologise in the first place. After all, life is about making little agreements and keeping them.'

If you're repeatedly late and always finding yourself apologising for it, then perhaps you need to hold yourself to account and change your behaviour.

When we regularly apologise for things but don't change our behaviour, we're not getting out of BED. If you don't take accountability, the issue will just get bigger and bigger. It's easy to make excuses and not take responsibility, but the result of that is people actually putting more time and effort into creative excuse-making than they do into taking accountability.

There are no excuses.

I was doing a university course and I got Covid. I had an essay due and one of my classmates said, 'Just contact the tutor and get an extension, mate. You've been sick.'

I said, 'I'm not making any excuses. I'm getting on with it.' I submitted it on time.

The fundamental thing for me isn't the apology, it's about not putting yourself in a position where you have to apologise. Ultimately, I want to encourage behavioural change.

Let's stop apologising. It just gives us elbow room for our poor choices.

Show gratitude

With a lot of clients I talk about being consciously aware of safeguarding yourself. That's really important. Something someone says will trigger them and the negative self-talk will start up. It's human nature that we focus on our mistakes and not on the things we get right. We can allow one negative thing to define us.

To change that, I encourage everyone to say thank you more often and to really acknowledge when other people do something good. We all want to be affirmed, so when you say thank you to someone, you can change the trajectory of their day or their life. You might never know the impact that you have on them, and it won't cost you anything.

I love being able to acknowledge and celebrate the success of my clients, and I know they really appreciate it. Likewise, it means the world to me when I get acknowledged, when a client thanks me for what I've done for them. That is absolutely fulfilling. You can debate the altruistic versus the egotistic, and I'll be the first to admit that I'm egotistical. I love that acknowledgement, and I genuinely want it – when I know I've earned it.

I've got a client who has moved to America. I got a card from her that said, 'To Dave, thank you so much for all your help. I really appreciate everything and how you tell it exactly like it is. It's been great to work with you and I know it's just the beginning. I feel so much more confident not just in my swimming but in myself.'

There's nothing better than getting that kind of thanks. It's got such power to it.

The effect of a comment, a smile, an acknowledgement … that's a contribution to this planet. We teach people how to treat us, and each other.

Do what you can, because it causes a ripple effect. Imagine if everyone did all the small things they could. That would be huge!

My grandad always shared compliments with people and I've modelled that from him. Whenever we went out he'd say things to Grandma like, 'You look absolutely lovely in that dress!' (He was a charmer!) But the smile he'd get back was magic. I loved seeing that.

There's something about exchanging positive energy that I've always enjoyed. I'll always try to engage in conversations in a way that leaves some nice, positive energy with people. When that's delivered genuinely, people really pick up on and appreciate it. When it's not genuine, it can have the opposite effect, so you're wasting your own and everyone else's time.

There's a great story about the Buddha, which talks about not responding to aggression with aggression. He asked, 'If you buy a gift for someone and that person does not accept it, to whom does the gift belong?'

It belongs to you. The same goes for anger, hostility, fake compliments and insults. If the person they're being given to – or aimed at – doesn't accept them, they continue to belong to the person doing the giving. All they are doing is hurting themselves.

The opposite is also true. If you give someone a genuine compliment and they don't want to take it, then it still belongs to you. If it's genuine and given with good grace, then whether they accept it or not is of no importance.

If I give a genuine compliment and the person doesn't want to take it that way, that's their problem and I'm not going to be affected by it or take it personally. In my experience, 99.99 per cent of the time it's been accepted and reflected.

Think about when you're having a rough time and someone says something nice. It really makes a difference. We could change the world with that.

Giving back

I truly believe that the only true way to wealth is to help others get what they want. That's why I do what I can to give back. There were so many people who helped me along the way in my career, so I see this as a way of paying it forward and a way of being respectful to and acknowledging those who have been there to support me. I know how important that support network and those sources of confidence have been to me along the way.

I've benefitted from various kinds of support, from people spending a lot of time with me to something as seemingly small as a comment from someone I respected.

That evening when I spoke at the Las Vegas event with Jim Rohn, all he said to me was, 'You have a bright future ahead of you.' He will never know the impact that had on me.

The stranger sitting next to me that day could have said exactly the same thing to me, and I'd have appreciated it and thanked them, but it wouldn't have had a lasting impact on me. But when you have someone of significance, who you've idolised, acknowledging you, that's massive.

There are so many ways, big and small, to give back. When I hear people bitching and moaning about things happening in their community, I usually think, *What have you done to contribute to changing that?* By holding yourself to account and taking responsibility, you can make a massive difference in this world.

If you've been involved in team sport – especially rugby and rugby league – you'll probably have noticed that there's always a mother-hen character in every one of those clubs. The mother hen is someone who should be listened to, because the mother hen always has common sense and wisdom. They'll check up on the little things, like making sure everyone knows where they need to be and when, and keeping people in line with a quick, 'Hey! You take your hat off when you come in, please!' They uphold some beautiful values, and that's powerful – both in its execution and in the role-modelling they're doing for youngsters.

There are people like that in every community and they're awesome people. They're often unsung heroes. If you know one, thank them. If your community doesn't have one, become one.

I do my bit by sitting down with young kids to inspire them to be better, and I'm doing that because I care about my community.

As part of that process of giving back, I've set up my own foundation. Through it, I find individuals who can't afford my coaching but who have passion, attitude, potential and a willingness to put the work in, and I'll invest in them, in part because I had such good mentors, who really cared about me. It gives me a real buzz if I can help someone and I love being able to do that. One of those athletes was Paralympian Tupou Neiufi. I just knew she had something special, and she sure went on to prove it, by winning a gold medal in the pool at the Tokyo Paralympics.

PROFILE

Drive and passion

Tupou Neiufi

Swimmer

- Paralympics debut in Rio, 2016, at age 15
- Silver medallist 100m backstroke S8, World Para Swimming Championships, 2019
- Gold medallist 100m backstroke S8, Paralympics, 2020
- Silver medallist 100m backstroke S8, Commonwealth Games, 2022
- Bronze medallist 100m backstroke S8, World Para Swimming Championships, 2023

When Tupou was just a toddler, a hit-and-run outside her home left her with paralysis on the left side of her body. Her injuries were so bad that she had to relearn basic skills like sitting and using her arms.

When she went to school, she was keen to play netball but found it difficult to keep up. Instead, on the recommendation of her physiotherapist, she turned her attention to swimming. She started competing at the age of 10 and was soon identified as a potential champion by Paralympics New Zealand.

Tupou comes from a large Tongan family; she's the eldest of seven children. I could see that she had huge drive and was really passionate about swimming.

Together, we worked on her being able to create strategies to overcome stress and anxiety when going into competitions, and to find self-confidence not only as an athlete but within herself as a person. Tupou also wanted to work on her communication skills, as she knew that they would be important in the role she would play. I was so proud of her for always wanting to upskill and put herself out there.

She is a very humble young lady, and I don't know if she had even dreamed about going to the Paralympics, so getting there for her was incredible.

In an interview with Newsroom's Rebecca Dubber in 2019, she showed the true hallmarks of someone with the winning mindset.[3]

While it's the right decision for her swimming, Neiufi admits she misses the social aspect of school and seeing her friends.

'They'll text me and ask if I'm coming out, and I'll have to say no because of training or a swim meet. It's disappointing, but I'm focused on my swimming, and I have to prioritise that,' she says.

'But they'll text me before a meet to wish me luck. It's little things like that, that mean a lot to me.'

Ahead of the world championships, Neiufi wasn't focused on winning medals, but on improving her times and learning from the opportunity to compete.

'I always want to move forward; if I can improve my times then I know all the training and hard work I'm putting in is working, and that's enough for me. It would be nice to qualify a slot for Tokyo or win a medal, but that's not my sole focus,' she said.

Tupou sure did keep moving forward. She not only qualified for Tokyo, but she also won a medal – a gold one! Watching her swim and win that gold at Tokyo, Jo and I were both crying our eyes out. Seeing Tupou cry just made me cry. It was epic.

When she got home, she came to see me and even let me wear her gold medal! I was stoked to have the chance to tell her that I could not have been a prouder coach, having seen her transform into an exceptionally driven and focused young woman with such a beautiful, caring heart.

Chapter 6

AM I RIGHT OR AM I WINNING?

The importance of communication

I hate writing text messages. What's lost in a text is the tone in which it's intended, which can lead to people misinterpreting the words. I'll take a phone call over a text any time.

Similarly, given the choice between a phone call and an in-person meeting, I'll always choose to see someone in person. I want to be able to see their face, look at their reactions and observe their body language. All of that is important.

In neurolinguistic programming, we talk about there being three components to communication:

1. Spoken words
2. Tone of voice
3. Physiology or body language

Here's the interesting thing: words are only worth 7 per cent of the total message being conveyed and received. Tonality is worth 38 per cent and the remainder is all physiology. What that means is that, when you communicate with someone, they're basing their interpretation of your intentions and attitude 7 per cent on what you actually say, 38 per cent on the way you say it, and 55 per cent on what your face and body movements are expressing. So if you say to someone, 'I'm not angry at you,' while shouting, frowning and clenching your fists, the words themselves are not going to contradict all the other signals you're sending.

There are times when you've got to be practical, and talking to people on the phone or online is absolutely fine in a lot of cases – but it largely depends on what needs to be communicated. For me as a coach, I have clients online all around the world, but there's still nothing more powerful than a face-to-face conversation. I think there's something organic and real about a face-to-face conversation that can't be fully replicated by virtual alternatives.

What I'm looking for generally is incongruent behaviour, language or framing. If the words, tone and physiology that someone is using don't match up, it shows. How we communicate is predominately through our physiology. People will use words as a representation, but that's just a small part of the overall picture they're communicating.

Choose your words wisely

While spoken words make up only a small percentage of communication, it's still important to choose them wisely. There's something powerful in practising a conscious awareness of the words you use – both to yourself and to other people.

American radio host Bernard Meltzer is credited with saying, 'Before you speak, ask yourself if what you are going to say is true, is kind, is necessary, is helpful. If the answer is no, maybe what you are about to say should be left unsaid.' This is a sentiment that reflects some key teachings of the Ancient Greek philosophers, and it's one that is worth incorporating into your daily routines.

We all have long days and we all get tired. Instead of feeling sorry for yourself, get into the habit of interrupting that thought process and changing your energy. It's so easy to start off by having a bit of a whinge and it becoming habitual. If necessary, ask your partner or your friends to pull you up if they hear you getting into that negative space.

You've got to build your conscious awareness to get to a point where you don't start going down that rabbit hole, because it's there that you start reinforcing negative behaviours. If you have that self-awareness you can deploy strategies like your affirmations; being conscious of your energy puts a manhole cover over the rabbit hole and prevents you from dropping into it, and it helps keep you on an even keel.

Some people talk about mindfulness, but I prefer 'conscious attention'. You really do need to pay conscious attention to your words because they form the way you map the world, the way you frame your life and the limitations that you create for yourself. When you become aware of how you're channelling your energy, you can have a process where you take a moment to go, 'Hang on! Let's get a better perspective here.'

By challenging and changing the words you use, your perspective will change too. Doing this will help you to deal with and overcome any worries you might have, taking you another step in your lifelong journey towards creating that version of yourself that you are undoubtedly proud of.

Learn to say no

You should be confident in saying yes to some things and no to others. Doing that is aligned with having clarity and understanding your own core values, and it allows you to direct your energy so that you become very quick to recognise and call out people who are fake.

This is not to say that everything you believe is absolutely correct and it's what everyone else should believe. Believing that just makes you an arrogant prick. Having confidence in your convictions means that you will not compromise on the values that you truly believe in while keeping an open mind to the possibility of change.

When it comes to high-performance sport, one of the things I tell my clients is that they need to give themselves permission to be selfish. It's a requirement. They're going to have to say no to their mates, they're going to have to stand fast. Being committed as an athlete, you must be clear on your goals and do whatever it takes to reach them. You shouldn't ever feel that you need to justify your decisions when you say no. You shouldn't have to explain when you can't or don't want to do something.

I have no qualms about saying no. People ask me, 'Can I see you on Saturday?'

'No.'

'What times have you got available?'

'Monday to Thursday.'

'What about Friday?'

'No.'

A lot of people are so altruistic and wanting to please everyone else that they are incapable of saying no. You have to be able to say no. You have to be able to give yourself permission to put yourself first.

I think the word 'no' is one of the most beautiful words in the English language. If you give excuses instead of simply saying 'no', people are very quick to manipulate and talk you into doing something you don't want to do.

People who know me know that if I don't want to do something, I won't do it. At the same time, that's got to be balanced with a certain level of obligation. There are times when it's appropriate to do things that you don't want to do.

When you're too agreeable, you make the mistake of giving your power away, and people are very quick to take it from you. They'll grab your power and your energy as soon as you let them.

Engage in difficult conversations

Some people need to be tenacious and maintain a very strong self-image because, when they get success, everyone will be lining up for a share of their money. There can be people in their lives who will feel entitled to a pay cheque or for some part of whatever else they might have.

I had one client who was a young rugby league player. He was facing all sorts of demands on his finances, assets and time, and he was having trouble managing them all. I said, 'Mate, can you guarantee that you won't be injured next season?'

His answer was no.

My next question was, 'If you are injured – let's just say you break your leg – what are you going to do then?'

He said he didn't know.

'Are you going to be playing rugby league for the rest of your life, then retiring at 67, like people in "normal" jobs do?'

No way!

Many high-performance athletes have a time limit on their careers. Whatever they earn during this window of opportunity has to serve them, their partner, their children and whoever else in their families they support. When their sporting career is over, the money they earn from it will stop too, so they need to plan for their post-retirement future.

Sometimes, what I say can clash with some of their cultural ideals, but managing other people's expectations of them is important. The people who expect things of these sportspeople don't stop to consider that a playing career – and therefore a level of income – won't last forever.

These can be tricky conversations, but it's important that they're approached respectfully and framed in a way that doesn't feel like judgement.

I have another client, who had just got himself an NRL contract when we had a similar conversation about finances and his longevity in the game. He ended up saying, 'Thanks bro, because I've woken up to that stuff, but no one else would dare to say that for fear of offending me.' That goes back to my very first question: 'Do you give me permission to be blunt and honest with you?'

My clients come and, yes, I will ask them to give me permission to be blunt and honest. But I also reinforce the fact that our time together is a safe place. Anything that clients share with me will never leave the four walls of my office.

Part of what I need to do as a coach is to navigate through various – and sometimes deeply held – biases in a way that gives my clients space to ponder in a way that they don't feel threatened. The only way you can do that is by having built a high level of respect and rapport. It's a bit of a fine art, but when done successfully it can have a huge effect on an individual's outlook and their overall success.

There's real power in a justified, truthful belief, and that's what needs to be brought to the fore in those hard conversations. To counter any argument they might put forward in a way that's not dismissive or disrespectful, you need to have a strong self-image. Standing up to people who may not have your best interests at heart, and standing fast with your convictions, is all part of having the winning mindset.

The last thing I want to be accused of is trying to convince people to move away from their own faith and come to another sense of faith. I want to be respectful of that, while having an obligation to help the people I work with to achieve their dreams.

When I'm giving you advice, I'm not emotionally attached. I'm not part of your family. I am purely here because you've made a statement about what you want, so I am going to hold you to account and give you guidance in achieving that. That means, for the majority of the time, what I'll be giving you is good stuff, but there may be conversations that will be rather uncomfortable. There are times when those conversations need to be had.

This is especially likely when I'm dealing with young people who are trying to navigate through high-performance and professional sport. For a lot of them, it's a case of 'you don't know what you don't know'. Often they'll feel like they're part of the herd. If everyone is doing something, they think it must be OK, but that's not necessarily the case.

They're not always thinking about the things that might go wrong. They're enthusiastically thinking about the game, the money and the opportunities. Sometimes, you have to be the bearer of bad news and give them a sense of perspective. That's one of the ways I will hold people to account.

The importance of discourse

I love the art of debate. I believe in free speech, but there should be rules of engagement so people don't disrespect each other. I love having conversations with people who think differently from me. I like being enlightened. I like trying to understand why people think the way they do.

We tend to seek out people who confirm our biases, but we need to talk more to people whose opinions differ from ours. I ask a lot of questions, because it helps me to understand why people think the way they do.

People don't often unpack, consider or confront their own beliefs. They might be forced to do it in certain situations, but on the whole it doesn't happen much. I think investigating your own underlying biases and beliefs is a really healthy thing to do, because it helps you to understand how you respond to things. I'm fascinated by how people come to create their beliefs and their thoughts.

The ability to have discourse in an organised and respectful way seems to be disappearing. Now differences of opinion seem to quickly descend into a shit fight to see who can scream the most. It's pathetic.

With social media, the concern that I have is: where is the truth? The gift we had in the past was that the only source of information was the news. Even then it was filtered through the biases and viewpoints of the companies and journalists who prepared and presented it, but today everyone's an expert and everyone can always find someone to agree with them.

We should be able to disagree with each other without it becoming a shouting match. Maybe we need to reinvent debating. Maybe we need to learn how to talk to each other again. We definitely need to learn to think about where our information comes from, and to think more critically. We need to question who benefits from us believing what is being said.

We need to open up channels of communication in a mature, methodical, structured way that allows us to speak and to be heard, and that allows us to agree to disagree without it becoming a slanging match.

Agree to disagree

When you have a strong self-image, you're not intimidated by others, nor are you influenced by them. You can appreciate opinions. You can dissociate emotionally from situations without being triggered. You're confident to agree to disagree.

I want to have a discussion at a level of discourse that is professional and respectful. More importantly, I want the outcome of this kind of conversation to have effect – to make some level of change. It's not just about being right.

A lot of people are far too agreeable in the sense that, in order to keep the peace, they'll just agree. That does damage as well. If you can agree to disagree through a good dialogue, then you both maintain each other's respect.

As Stephen R Covey wrote in *The Seven Habits of Highly Effective People*: 'Seek first to understand then to be understood.'

Rather than disagreeing with someone, try to find out why they think what they think. Sometimes, in that conversation, they might realise that their opinion has a flawed basis.

A lot of people get confused about how they're supposed to operate and what's appropriate. Part of that is cultural. There are certain factors from a cultural perspective that I need to be mindful of so that I don't infringe on other people's beliefs. Just because we think differently doesn't mean I can't work with someone who has different beliefs than I do. I appreciate people who have conviction in their beliefs, but I expect them to appreciate that I have the conviction of my own beliefs too.

I'll be upfront and frame up where I'm at with an example. I had one client who I became very good friends with. When you think about religion, you probably couldn't get two people whose views differed more extremely. She was really worried about that and, to be honest, I was too. But we just agreed to disagree while still respecting each other. That is so important.

I have another good friend who is more of a spiritual person than me. I've read a lot of texts about Christianity and various religions, and I said to my friend, 'Everything you read will confirm your biases.' I got him to come and hear Richard Dawkins speak. I told him he wouldn't agree with what was said, but I asked him to have an open mind. Wow! We opened up channels of communication through that experience. We both agree to respect each other's boundaries and our discussions are really frank. It's great.

Be open to changing your mind

Human beings are quick to hold onto a belief system. With today's media and electronic devices, we can get information instantly. The challenge we have now is in figuring out how to know if what we're reading or seeing is true.

Before we jump to any conclusion, there has to be a certain amount of investigation. We've also got to appreciate that we all have biases within us and those biases will generally influence how we seek, consume and retain information.

Hearing from someone who thinks differently to the way you do can reinforce your beliefs or it can challenge them. Neither of those things is bad.

The issue we have today is that we're very submissive beings. Nietzsche talked about the herd. Most people will be part of the herd – camels who are very quick to say 'yes, that's the truth'. And yet, with investigation, sometimes we might find out that what we were told isn't the truth – and that's OK. In order to progress from being a camel to being a lion, you have to have the courage to question.

Whenever a belief we hold is challenged, we tend to get defensive, dig in and fight. We will shut down. We will shout so we don't have to listen to what the other person is saying. We are unable to sit with the discomfort of what we're hearing. If another person is screaming at you, and you can be articulate, assertive and calm under fire, you've already won the argument to a certain point.

If something makes us feel uncomfortable, we should investigate it. What is it about what we're experiencing that makes us feel uncomfortable? *Why* does it make us feel uncomfortable? Was the other person's intent to make us uncomfortable? If not, what *was* their intent?

I had one client who I worked with for three years. She was a business owner, and in that whole time she never brought an agenda to one of our sessions. By the end of that time, she wasn't coming because she needed my help; she was coming because she wanted to have her thinking and her biases challenged. Business owners especially love that because for them sometimes it's a case of, who motivates the motivated? When you're the boss, who's questioning you? At the end of that three years of coaching, we were able to look back and realise how much she'd grown and changed.

It's the businesspeople who sometimes get the most out of me being blunt and honest with them. If it's required, I will push their buttons over a statement they make or a belief they hold that potentially could be contaminated.

Sometimes those beliefs and feelings, are justified, but sometimes they also need to be challenged in some way because of the effect they have on the person's physiology and neurology. I'll ask, 'How does that help you? How does it serve you?'

Am I right or am I winning?

We've all said certain things about certain people that we know we shouldn't have said. I say terrible things about Queensland rugby league teams and State of Origin referees, but that's not intellectual, it's just emotion.

If we respond to things with our intellect, we can do so with poise. Today, we're so defensive and reactive that we'll respond to things out of emotion instead of intellect. How many times have you had a text message or email that's annoyed you, and you've sat there and immediately typed out a response? If you've sent those responses, how often have they got you the resolution you were hoping for?

Not often, I'd guess.

If, however, you've written that draft, then put it aside for a bit and come back to it, how often have you sent it unchanged?

Not often, I'd guess.

The question to ask in these situations is: Am I right or am I winning?

Most people operate from wanting to be right. For me, personally, I like to win. There are times when I may be right, but disempowering the other person or embarrassing them will mean that I'm not really winning, so I'll change the approach with that in mind. Being aware of the difference and understanding where your priorities are is a great way to filter communication.

You might be right, but are you winning? By all means, write that draft, but do it in a place where there's no chance of you accidentally sending it. Open a new email and write it there. Scribble it down on a piece of paper. Write it in the notes on your phone. Just don't accidentally send it before you've had time to ask yourself the question, and respond once the initial emotion has calmed down.

We have bias built in, so we see things only from our perspective. The key is having enough intellectual intuition to know when it's important to apply that, and when you're just wasting your time and you should move on.

We all need to take a pause sometimes so we can have a think about how to respond in the appropriate context.

When someone is being disrespectful, that's when it's about being right. There are other times when you need to rise above, and that's when it's about winning.

You teach people how to treat you. Don't spend time dwelling on people who don't treat you well. They're robbing you of your energy and time, and they don't care about that. Be aware of your emotional response when someone infringes your core values, but don't let it be the only thing that informs how you respond to them.

Choose your battles

You've got to be mindful of the things that are worthy of investigation. You've got to be able to assess what is worth spending your time on.

People are happy to be online warriors and say things they'd never say to someone's face. If someone makes a comment that you disagree with, you've got two options. You can challenge them and have an argument, or you can just let it go.

The first rule of discourse is to never argue with an idiot. If I know that I'm not going to get anywhere in the discussion, I'll just keep my mouth shut. I won't waste my energy.

You've got to choose your battles. I see people making comments on social media, then there'll be this massive chain of conversation that goes nowhere. The time it took those people to write all that stuff, they could have gone for a run, gone to the gym, had a swim, played with their dog, read a chapter of a book, hugged their kids or told someone that they're beautiful. All of those things could have made a positive difference in the world.

Instead, they choose to get angry at someone they probably don't even know and may well never meet. More importantly, when all that's been said and done, what's changed? Nothing.

When it comes to arguing with people online, I'd remind you of something Nietzsche said: 'Beware that, when fighting monsters, you yourself do not become a monster … for when you gaze long into the abyss, the abyss gazes also into you.'

Avoid gossip

When it comes to conversation, I love this quote from Eleanor Roosevelt: 'Poor minds talk about people. Average minds talk about events. Great minds talk about ideas.'

I love the stimulation that comes from engaging in conversations about ideas. In fact, I love it so much that most Friday mornings I have my Breakfast of Champions. I invite all sorts of different people to come and have breakfast with me at my favourite café. They might be sports champions, psychologists, psychotherapists or successful businesspeople – I just really enjoy the stimulating conversations that we have.

You don't need to sit down with a bunch of interesting people in order to engage with mind-expanding ideas – just turn your phone or TV into a classroom instead of wasting your time gossiping or listening to other people gossip.

When I'm around people who are gossiping and talking about nonsense, I get bored with the conversation. That goes back to the principle of protecting yourself at all times; of assigning importance to valuing yourself and your time. I am very selective and I won't allow anyone to steal time from me. The moment that someone starts gossiping with me, it's an indication that I don't think I'll be spending a lot of time with them.

I often call people out when they start to gossip in social situations. I'll ask, 'Why are you so interested in that? How does that affect you?'

Their usual response is to get embarrassed.

If you find people around you are gossiping, ask yourself whether they have a loving intent and a desire to help. If not, then perhaps you should reconsider the time you invest in them.

Again, the best way to deal with that is through the Buddha's teaching: if someone wants to give you a gift, and you choose not to accept it, to whom does the gift belong? It belongs to the person who tried to give it to you.

If someone wants to give you abuse, gossip or unkindness, and you choose not to accept it, that stuff belongs to them, not you.

Protect yourself at all times. Don't let people pollute your life, steal your time and drain your energy just because that's what you've always done, or because you fear how they might react, or because it scares you to speak up.

Chapter 7

YOUR EMOTIONAL TOOLBOX

Your emotional toolbox contains a series of mental strategies to help you cope more effectively in any given situation. I want to introduce you to a series of strategies that I've used over the years to help my athletes get the best out of themselves and become more consistent with their performance.

The zone

Within high-performance sport, you'll often hear people talking about being 'in the zone'.

Your ability to get into that zone can depend on your state of mind. There are three key states that people get into when responding to stress, each of which will be reflected in their communication. They are:

1. Aggressive – hostile, alienates others, causes conflict, uses defensive body language
2. Assertive – confident, honest, respectful, relaxed body language, will make eye contact
3. Passive – ignores own needs, allows others to take the lead, avoids conflict, won't make eye contact

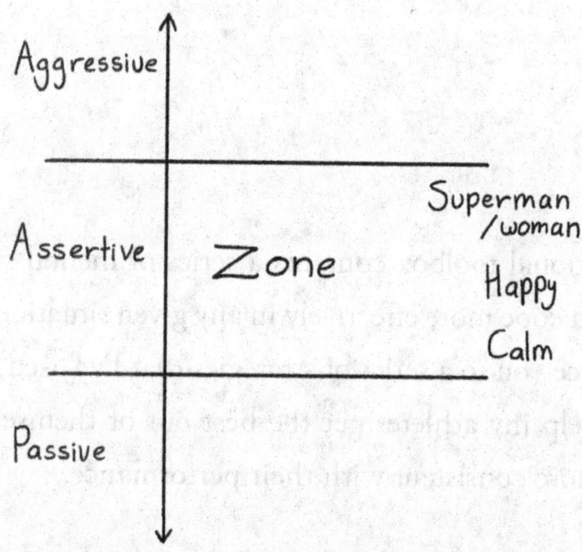

When we are in passive or aggressive states, we are not in the zone for peak performance. Neurologically, those states relate to the fight, flight or freeze stress responses. These are reactions our body has when our brain perceives that we are in danger. They evolved to deal with life-threatening events, but now whenever we're feeling stress, our brain can quickly tell the body to fight, run away (flight) or freeze and do nothing. The fight response is aggressive, while the flight and freeze responses are passive. When you're in any of these states, your body releases adrenaline and cortisol to help give you the boost it needs to fight or run away.

In any of those situations, it's about decision-making and clarity of mind. We don't make good decisions when we're angry. The key thing here is the management of your emotional state and understanding that your state is a choice.

Most people are either aggressive or passive, but to be 'in the zone' you need to be assertive. When you are in this assertive state, you are in the performance window.

The performance window

Within the performance window, there are three states:

1. Calm
2. Happy
3. Übermensch/superman/superwoman

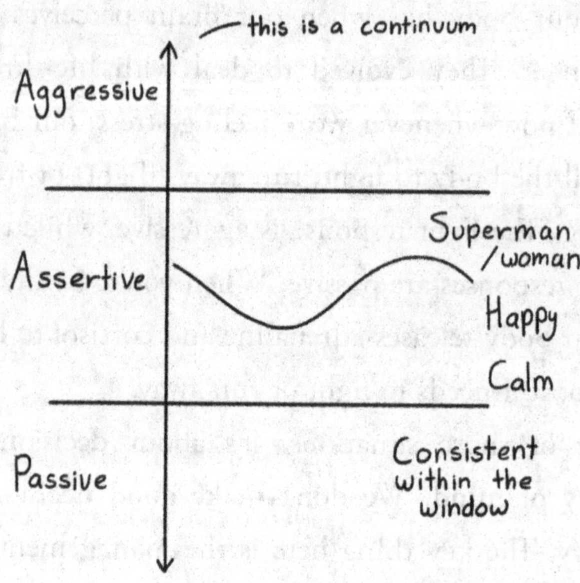

Calm

Of them, calm is the foundation. If you can only be one state in that window, be calm.

The best tool to help you become calm is your breathing. By using your breathing, you can counter those stress hormones and set your physiology.

EXERCISE

Breathing

If you're getting a little anxious, the best place to start is your breathing. I teach a four-five-slow method:

- Breathe in through the nose while you count to four
- Hold the breath while you count to five
- Breathe out slowly through your mouth
- Repeat until you notice a difference in your physiology

This helps to reduce the stress response hormones, which allows you to then get into a physiological state that moves you away from focusing on trying to cope and moves you towards being calm and clear-minded with your behaviours and your choices.

Happy

Next is a happy state. The reason I talk about being in a happy state is because when you're happy, when your eyes are above the plane of the horizon, it's virtually impossible to access negative feelings and self-talk. If you can't access those feelings, you're more likely to perform well.

The old saying 'chin up' has some real power in it. If your chin goes up, your eyes go up.

Remember that the body and mind are connected, and the body responds to your thoughts. If you start going down that negative rabbit hole, your physiological state will reflect that. What do you do if you recognise that you're having that negative thought? The first thing I'd suggest you do is change your physiology.

Remember that in neurolinguistic programming, words are only worth 7 per cent of the overall message, tonality is worth 38 per cent and the remainder is all physiology. So if you want to get bang for your buck, adjusting your physiology allows you to be more effective in adjusting your internal representation and your language.

When we have an appropriate physiological state, it has a huge impact on the internal representation of feelings.

Don't get me wrong: I'm OK with emotions, including negative ones like anger. We need to express them – but at the appropriate time. For athletes, that's at the end of the game. While we're in the game, we're going to get a little angry here and there, but let's navigate that to stay focused on getting the job done. Afterwards, debrief with your coaching team.

EXERCISE

Change your physiological state

Become aware of how you stand, walk and sit – then make the adjustment. Hold your head up, put your shoulders back, keep your eyes above the horizon. Your perspective will change with your posture.

I want you to stand up straight. Put your feet together. Leave your hands at your sides. Look up to the ceiling. Put a big smile on your face. Now, without changing anything, I want you to get sad. Don't move your feet, don't drop your head and, most importantly, keep smiling. Try to lean into those negative feelings.

You can't do it. In order to get sad, the first thing you would have to do is change your physiology.

The power of images

One athlete I worked with used to draw a little smiley face on her hand before she went into competition. She loved that representation of being happy, and it helped her to perform better. When she was in that happy state, that changed her physiology, her internal representation and her focus.

Übermensch/alter ego

The last state within the performance window is the Übermensch, or superman or woman. The term Übermensch was first coined by Nietzsche in 1883. Its literal translation is 'overman', but it has come to mean a person who has such incredible powers that they seem to be superhuman.

This state is more difficult to access, but having first become calm (through breathing) and happy (through changing your physiological state), that is when you can ignite that alter ego and really go into superhuman mode.

When it comes to really overcoming some of their limiting beliefs, developing an alter ego has been one of the biggest breakthroughs with a lot of my athletes. With a lot of my fighters, I talk about being in that state of the alter ego, which, ultimately, means being absolutely fearless. When you become fearless, that is freedom. It doesn't guarantee outcome, but it improves possibility and probability – and that's huge in life.

When I was doing Strongman and powerlifting, my alter ego was a bull. My opponents could either face 146kg David Niethe or a 1000kg raging bull. Which one would you rather deal with?

Developing an alter ego

The development of an alter ego requires something kids use all the time – imagination.

The best way to understand the process is for me to tell you a story. I had a weightlifting coach contact me to see if I could help out one of his athletes. He said she had everything she needed to be a champion – except self-belief.

Tracey Lambrechs was preparing for the Commonwealth Games when she came to see me. We talked about the alter ego and how it might work for her. I took her through a process of using her imagination to find something meaningful to her that represented strength and power. She took me back to her childhood in South Africa.

I said, 'What do you see?'

'This majestic lion.'

I said, 'Good. Now I want you to manifest and walk into being the lion. I want you to think about the lion – its majestic mane and commanding, dominant presence. How does the lion, king of the plains, hold itself? With grace and pure strength.'

She really got herself into the skin of that majestic lion and it became her alter ego.

She qualified to go to the Commonwealth Games. She wasn't expected to do well there, but she ended up with a bronze medal. Afterwards, she said to me, 'Dave, I felt like a lion.'

She went from Tracey Lambrechs, saying, 'I hope I do alright …' to that strong, powerful lioness, who was capable of anything. By changing her attitude, perception and thinking, she achieved huge things.

For me, it was bittersweet. I think it was sweet in the sense that she got bronze, but it was bitter in the sense that, if she'd come to see me earlier, I possibly could have pushed her further up the podium!

The power of the alter ego is that, when we lack confidence, we can put it on and get into that ultimate state of the superhuman.

Perhaps the most famous alter ego out there is the Stylebender, which is an idea I worked with Israel Adesanya to create. I recognised early on that Israel's whole body language would change when he started talking about anime. When he started talking about *Avatar: The Last Airbender*, I could see his whole physiology change. I told him I wanted him to play with that.

The show featured characters based around the four elements – airbenders, waterbenders, earthbenders and firebenders. These characters were all able to use their minds to control their specific element, which in the show is called 'bending'. Each element's bending used a style of martial arts devised especially for them.

As we talked about an alter ego, he landed on 'the Last Stylebender', which was then shortened to just Stylebender. Now, who would you rather fight – Israel, who is mortal, or the Stylebender, who has superpowers?

As Izzy gets taped up before going into a fight, he goes through a transformation. He becomes the Stylebender. When he does that, what he brings into the ring is sometimes more than the sum of all its parts.

The alter ego is the ultimate hack. We hack into our brain and we can get rid of all the historical bullshit and fast-track ourselves to a state of immediate action. We can use it to override any limiting belief or perception.

It also allows you to protect something of yourself that you're not giving to the public. You're applying a filter to yourself that dampens any potential perception of stress or expectation. Believing *When I'm in this state, I become truly fearless* means negative comments and thoughts don't have the potential to contaminate that confidence. It's almost like putting on a protective shield. People can throw all the abuse they want, but it just slides off that shield.

Alter ego is applicable in the sense that it allows you to manage your physiology, because you are in a place where your intentions and attention come into alignment. When they're in alignment, that affects your behaviour.

A lot of people have intentions, but they're not quite there because their attention isn't in alignment with the outcome. When you align those two things, it becomes very powerful.

When you have an undoubtable belief in yourself, that puts you at peace. In that space, you're limiting any contaminating thoughts or feelings or perceptions. That's when you can put forward the best version of you, and that's all. It doesn't guarantee a win, but it certainly improves the probability of putting forward the best possible version of yourself.

You might not win, but you'll walk away feeling good about yourself. There will be many times when you *don't* win, but you'll feel bloody proud of yourself and your performance. If you're constantly programming that, imagine how quickly you can accelerate the progression of the development.

I can accelerate the development of an individual at a higher rate by using all these tools. That's a real buzz.

Another great example of someone who has created and used an alter ego to their advantage is the Australian UFC fighter Tyson Pedro. Tyson lives in Sydney, but he was over in Auckland training with the guys at City Kickboxing when someone suggested he come to see me.

Straight away, he was really interesting in the alter ego, and he really engaged with the concept. For him what resonated was the idea of being a rōnin, a type of samurai warrior who has no master but himself.

After his first-round knockout of Anton 'The Pleasureman' Turjkal at UFC 293 in September 2023, Tyson's celebration mimicked the moves of a samurai warrior. This led to questions at the post-fight press conference, where Tyson explained his motivation:

'I've been working with David Niethe in New Zealand, and we created this alter ego of becoming the Rōnin. As I was walking out to the cage, I was the calmest I've ever been. I've replayed it over and over again in my head. When we were doing the weight cuts we were listening to this samurai music. You know that scene from *The Last Samurai* where Katsumoto comes in with his crew … through the mist and there's dew on the grass. You can hear the horses and the heavy breathing, and you can feel the fear of the men. I just felt that when I was weight cutting.

'Then I stood up after cutting weight and I just felt that

celebration. When I did it, I saw my opponent at my feet. It was exactly how it played in my head – that moment in front of the home crowd. I don't know what's going to be able to beat that for a while to come. The crowd was behind me. I did that for my people. I did that for my family and it was one of the best moments of my sporting career.'

What the alter ego is not

People using the alter ego in this way differ from those people who project something other than their true selves on social media. The alter ego should be used in the context of performance and requirement. It is not a social experiment. It's not about comparing yourself socially, or about personal branding and inauthenticity for an audience.

There's always a payoff for behaviour, and the biggest need of an individual is to be affirmed and acknowledged, but depending on likes and followers for this external affirmation creates a false economy.

Imagine going online. You post something, and one of the things that confirms or motivates you to continue to post will be the fact that you've got a whole lot of likes. But you probably don't even know half of the people that follow you or like your posts. Why does their opinion matter? It doesn't. But despite their opinions being ultimately meaningless, their attention affirms you and gives you a sense of importance.

Unfortunately, collectively everybody is on there, and because that's how we often mistakenly measure worth, a lot of people don't recognise just how stupid it is to assign value to online popularity.

Outside the performance window

If you find yourself operating outside of the performance window, the first thing to remember is that you cannot change anything that you don't first recognise. In order to change your situation, you have to consciously acknowledge that you're outside the window.

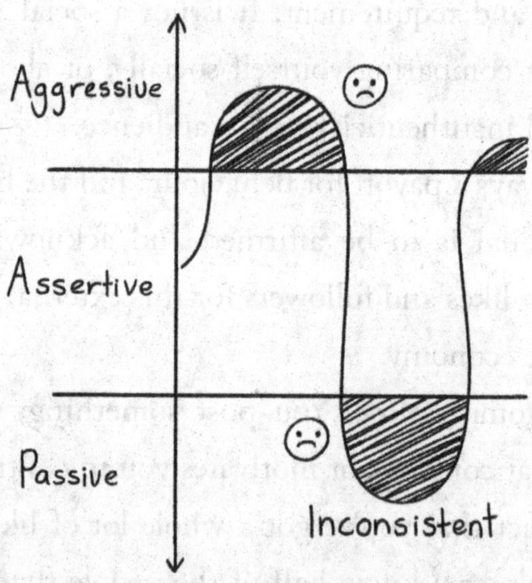

Once you've recognised what's going on, you need to deploy strategies to get yourself back into the right state. The first of these is breathing. Go into the four-five-slow exercise (page 156)

and do it as often as you need to in order to help reset your neurology. If you still find yourself outside of the performance window, it's time to 'act as if'. For example, if you don't feel confident, act as if you're confident, because that will provide you with the best opportunity to prove yourself and create the best version of yourself in that situation.

We all have days when we're absolutely on fire and days when we're not. If you don't recognise when you're having a not-so-good day, those days have the potential to contaminate the good ones. Self-awareness here is key, followed by deploying strategies for change.

If need be, add the affirmation 'I make good decisions' to your arsenal. That will become a programme playing in the background, which will help you to recognise when you're not in the right frame of mind.

Perspective and perceptional positioning

Today, a lot of people get told, 'Don't be a dreamer.' But I want to encourage that. I want you to dream and I want you to dream more effectively and visualise more effectively.

The observatory is one of my favourite places. I've always been fascinated by the universe, which is one of the reasons I am very big on the power of perspective. They say astronauts change dramatically because they get a dramatically different sense of perspective when looking down on Earth from space.

The term for this is 'the overview effect', and it was first written about by space writer Frank White in 1987.

In a 2018 interview with Yasmin Tayag of *Inverse*, NASA astronaut Nicole Stott said, 'I do remember initially looking out the window the first couple of days and wanting to see my home, wanting to see Florida from space. Finally, we were flying over Florida. I wanted to fly to the window and see it, and then realized somewhere down the line that I wasn't looking at Florida that same way anymore. I still wanted to see Florida, but Florida had just become this special part of home, which is Earth. I don't know when that happened. Was that two days after I got there? I mean, it wasn't like one day I woke up and was like, 'Oh yeah, Earth's my home.'

'It's a feeling of interconnectivity that you sometimes just don't get when you're in the middle of something. I think separating ourselves from things that are important to us is good because you then appreciate it in a new way. That definitely happened for me with Earth.'[4]

EXERCISE

Finding perspective

If you're feeling overwhelmed, ask yourself this question:

In terms of being anxious right now, where are you on a scale of one to ten?

Let's say, for the sake of this exercise, your answer is nine.

Now close your eyes and imagine you're floating up above your body, looking down on yourself.

Where are those feelings of anxiety now on that scale of one to ten?

You'll probably find they will have dropped a little – perhaps to a seven.

Now, with your eyes closed, imagine yourself flying all the way up through the clouds, out of the Earth's atmosphere, up towards the moon. Now you're flying past the moon, further and further out into space. Imagine turning around and looking back all the way past the planets, down to Earth. Think about what you can see, hear and feel.

Where are those feelings of anxiety now on that scale of one to ten?

Usually, the reply here is zero.

Now anchor into that feeling, really experience what it feels like to not be anxious. Then slowly bring your attention back to where you are, while still retaining that feeling of calm and perspective.

That process of visualisation like the one in the above exercise is called perceptional positioning. It's a pretty powerful tool to open the gateway for investigation. You can't carry out any investigation if you're stressed out.

As the subconscious mind has no idea of reality or time, we go forward to visualise the desired event and observe it taking place. When I go through the visualisation process with clients, there are two ways I get them to imagine things:

1. From the perspective of watching themselves from above the body – this reinforces the scene and visually confirms technical competency. Technically, you can see yourself doing those things.
2. Then I get them to drop down and see the event through their own eyes – this gives them the emotional information they need and allows them to grab the feelings and the beliefs associated with the event.

By helping people to visualise things from outside of their own body, it helps them to see in a way that is no longer one-dimensional. From both of these perspectives, I'll get them to go through an entire visual rehearsal of their competition.

Initially, try watching yourself in the event. When you visualise watching yourself in the event, I want you to focus on technical application and performance without engaging with the emotions that come with competing. Once you disengage as much of that emotion as possible, you can then move forward with mental clarity.

After that, you get to drop down into your body. In this state, engage your senses. Notice how things look, sound, taste, feel and smell. Really investigate the sensations.

From there, you take those feelings and the brain rewires the experience. The subconscious mind has no idea of the reality of time, so it thinks what you've just experienced is real. That builds belief in yourself.

This is something you'll see gymnasts and divers do a lot. They'll be on the side of the arena or at the bottom of the ladder, and you'll see them mentally rehearsing the routine or dive they're about to do. When they do this, they're also feeling their way through it. This helps to prepare them both mentally and physically for what they're about to do.

Afterwards, they'll feel more confident about their performance at the upcoming event. That's the power of visualisation.

Personality testing

If I had my time again, I would have spent some time investigating my personality earlier. I would have listened to what my Myers-Briggs type was and I might have avoided spending eight years being miserable as a printer. Having said that, maybe that in itself helped me because, at the time, I wasn't ready to engage in an intellectual way.

Your personality type can be found by completing a Myers-Briggs Type Indicator questionnaire. The indicators divide people according to four different categories: introversion or extraversion, sensing or intuition, thinking or feeling, and judging or perceiving.

The Myers-Briggs Type Indicator is a tool that has been outstanding in helping my clients succeed. I've had clients who want to focus on their career, and the next thing I know, they're looking at doing something completely different as a result of having investigated their personality type. I always tell people, 'Do what you are.' Any tool that helps you to get to know yourself, understand how you interact with people and discover what's important to you is great.

Knowing yourself and how you behave and react in social situations allows you to adapt your behaviour accordingly. Some people are very introverted, and sometimes it's necessary for them to be interactive, but at least they're aware that they need to make an effort to engage in conversations because it's good for business. It might not be ideal, but sometimes it's necessary. For that, they need to adapt.

The flipside of that is that they can plan to spend time by themselves to recharge their batteries after that social event.

During the consulting process, doing your Myers-Briggs Type Indicators gives me an idea of how you organise time. The system identifies people as either perceivers or judgers.

That is where I can get some idea if you're likely to be someone who tends to put things off.

We all perceive time differently. When people are in an accident, afterwards, when they're being interviewed, they often say, 'Oh my God, it happened so quickly.' While others will say, 'Time slowed down and I could see it coming.'

There are strategies we can use to counter that. I use timelines for visualisation and to improve a client's ability to access and be consciously aware of time more effectively.

The judger/perceiver scale in Myers-Briggs is helpful in eliciting timelines. For instance, when you imagine time, judgers are able to see the future and past in front of their eyes; they are likely to know what is present in a timely way, and they're time-conscious. A perceiver tends to store time differently, having the past behind them and the future in front. They lack time consciousness and run late.

When working with people who are very high on the perceiver scale who need to improve time organisation, turning their timeline 90° and running it in front of their eyes will help them understand both 'time' and 'being on time'.

Timelines

Another useful tool to help with anchoring perspective is through viewing your timeline. The field of timeline therapy was developed by Dr Tad James, who I trained with.

By timelines, I mean the entirety of a life. In neurolinguistic programming, your timeline is how your subconscious organises all your experiences and memories, as well as how it creates the experiences you want to have in the future.

In its simplest form, this can involve helping people realise that the average healthy person lives to, say, 80 years of age. Then I'll ask them their age, and the reply might be 20. That's followed by the important question, 'How many more years do you want to waste? Because you still have another 60-odd years to live! You've got a long way to go – do you want to continue down this path?'

Most people, however, need a little more than that.

There are two ways that people usually think about their timeline. There are:

1. In time – seeing the past as being behind them, the now inside their body and the future in front of them.
2. Through time – seeing the now as being outside their body (usually just in front of them), and the rest of time, both past and future, running on a line, often from left to right.

Working out which one of these you are is significant because it will help you to understand why you do some things.

'In time' people tend to be more focused on what's happening in the now and are able to focus on experiences as they occur. They tend to be a little less ordered and more flexible when it comes to deadlines. 'Through time' people see time laid out in a clearer way, so they find it easier to plan and focus on the future. They tend to be more ordered and more deadline-driven.

Usually, the process of viewing your timeline is something that is facilitated; however, if you want to try the process yourself, I'll step you through it.

EXERCISE

Viewing your timeline

Sit up straight, close your eyes and take a nice, deep breath in for four through the nose, hold for five, and breathe out slowly through the mouth. The breathing sets the foundation, so it helps to be nice and rhythmic with it.

Be aware of the breath as you gradually relax your entire body. Start with your forehead, your eyebrows, your eyelids, your ears, your nose, your cheeks, your jaw – get rid of any tension as you go.

Work your way down the whole of your body, relaxing each part as you go. Let your arms and legs go loose and limp. Get rid of any tension in your stomach.

Imagine drifting out of your body, all the way up to a cloud. The cloud is in the shape of a chair. Imagine snuggling up into the chair. Imagine your past and seeing the files of the memories going all the way back to your first memories.

When you look forward, you can see all the memories you will make, way into the future. As you look at them, point to where you see the past coming from. Is it from above, behind you or beside you? (This is where you'll come to understand whether you're an 'in time' person or a 'through time' person.)

Now point all the way into the future.

As you look at the files of all the memories of the past and all the files of the future, look down at them and allow them to manifest themselves into a line.

That line is your timeline. You can personalise it. Some people see it as a lightning bolt, some people see it as a path – mine is a laser beam. It doesn't really matter what it is, but personalise it, make it something meaningful to you.

Now drift all the way back to a period of time when you felt absolutely proud of yourself. Watch yourself and see yourself proud and confident. Acknowledge yourself and feel good about that.

Drift all the way down. Enjoy that moment. Feel all the feelings of absolute pride and confidence, and anchor that into your system and enjoy it for what it is.

Now drift all the way up into your chair and come all the way along your timeline back to now.

Think of something wonderful in the future, and drift along your timeline to whatever that moment might be. As you look down, see it like it's real, like a movie.

When you're ready, drift down from your chair and be in that moment. Be aware of the feeling of confidence in seeing yourself achieve the things you want to achieve.

When you're ready, drift all the way up, back onto the chair.

Now, go further into your future. I'm going give you free licence to manifest whatever you want and to drop down into each event. You can imagine all sorts of things. With each one, allow yourself to drop down into it and experience it.

As you go further and further into your future, imagine that as you look towards the end of your timeline there's a beautiful sense of light as you move and drop down into wonderful events. Acknowledge that sense of light.

Drift all the way to the very end of your timeline. You can feel the warmth and love of that light. Look back on all of your timeline and have the most incredible feeling of success and fulfilment and bliss.

When you're ready, enjoy stepping into that light, feeling a real sense of pride, confidence, motivation and energy. As you enjoy that, start drifting all the way back to now.

> You can now feel your energy coming back into your feet, then up your body through your calves, your legs, your chest and all the way up to your head. Your eyes are starting to open and then your eyes are open and you're back in the room feeling wonderful in every way.

Quite often when I guide people through this exercise, they'll get emotional, and I'll see them having flashes of recognition. I know that they're constructing something really powerful in those moments. Because it's so powerful, the brain pays attention to it.

Doing this exercise regularly will help you stay focused on your goals. It will also help reinforce whatever it is that you've put on your vision board.

I want to reinforce goals and I want to act as if they're certainties and take people there. A lot of my athletes, I've taken them to that event they've seen themselves win. The subconscious mind has no idea between reality and imagination, so it starts building energy and belief. It starts to go, 'You know what? I really think that I can do this!' Then that confidence goes up.

These are the little one percenters. When you have that sort of energy and focus, it's not like it's dramatic shifts all at once, but every day that you go to the gym you've got a sense of purpose, and that's powerful.

There's nothing more exciting than knowing where you're going. It's like having a little secret. Most people, at some point, search for meaning and purpose in life. Once you put the time in to find out what yours is, then start working towards it, it feels great.

PROFILE

The power of the alter ego

Israel Adesanya

MMA fighter

- Professional boxing: 6 bouts, 5 wins, 1 by knockout*
- Kickboxing: 80 fights, 75 wins, 29 by knockout*
- MMA: 27 fights, 24 wins, 16 by knockout, 8 by decision*
- Signed to Ultimate Fighting Championship (UFC) December 2017
- UFC Fight Night debut against Rob Wilkinson, 11 February 2018
- UFC Newcomer of the Year 2018
- First two-time UFC Middleweight Championship winner: interim Middleweight title vs Kelvin Gastelum, April 2019, claimed undisputed title vs Robert Whittaker, 12 February 2022

---

* at time of writing

- Challenged for Light Heavyweight title vs Jan Blachowicz, 6 March 2021
- Reclaimed undisputed Middleweight title vs Alex Pereira, 8 April 2023
- New Zealand Sportsman of the Year 2019
- *Stylebender* documentary released 2023
- Currently ranked second in the UFC flyweight division

I first met Izzy in 2016 after one of the coaches at City Kickboxing told him to come and see me. He'd lost a couple of fights and needed a bit of direction.

I knew from the get-go that he was destined for greatness. Back then, Izzy had a good grasp on the power of the mind and what he was capable of, and he had an eagerness to take on board everything I threw at him. He was already well on the way to having the winning mindset.

Together, we worked on pinpointing the areas of his life that were not serving him. One of these was the fact that he was gradually burning himself down. Once these things were identified, we developed some new strategies and he was able to take a new approach to them.

During the coaching process, I was looking for micro changes, and from the moment he started talking about *Avatar: The Last Airbender*, I knew we were onto something. His eyes would light up and his physiology changed, so I knew this was where we had to focus.

I told him I wanted him to play with the idea of the characters who used elemental powers and who each had their own style of martial arts specific to them. That's how he came up with the idea of the Last Stylebender.

With Izzy, it was almost like I didn't have to do much because he was already on the right path. He already had a vision and big, unrealistic goals, which I encouraged. Some people just need that little affirmation, and he was one of them. Once we had worked on a few things, he took off very, very quickly.

Everything that we talked about – the goal-setting and the vision board – he got right into. On his vision board, he superimposed the UFC belt around his waist, and I don't even know if he had a UFC contract at the time. However, this was where I wanted his mind to be – exploring and being in an undoubtable state of belief in self: 'act as if'.

He was staying with Mike Angove, one of his coaches. Mike came home one afternoon and tiptoed into the house. The guys train three or four times a day, so they'll have a snooze whenever they can. As he tiptoed past Izzy's bedroom, he saw Izzy sitting on the end of the bed, looking up, saying, 'I'm middleweight champion of the world ...'

Within a couple of years, it was a reality. That just reinforces the power of the visual and the importance of the vision board. Any thought continuously held in the mind will soon seek expression through some practical means. It's the power of focus and the law of attraction.

I have a lot of clients. However, the one question I am always asked is, 'What is Izzy really like?'

I can honestly say he is the humblest of human beings with the kindest heart. He would give you the shirt off his back.

I know this because I have one of his shirts. Hanging on the wall of my office in a frame is Izzy's walk-out hoodie from UFC 236 – Adesanya v Gastelum – signed and blood-stained.

Izzy had gifted the hoodie to an auction raising funds for the Sudan Federation of Muaythai. The money raised went to help support and develop Sudanese teams and to pay travel costs for them to attend IFMA tournaments where they represented Sudan.

One thing I've heard him say often is, 'When I win, we all win.'

Chapter 8

THE MAP IS NOT THE TERRITORY

Making your brain work for you

Your brain is the most powerful tool you have when it comes to creating the life you want for yourself. A big part of having the winning mindset is about being conscious and deliberate in your thinking. If you can learn to make your brain work for you, the probability and the possibility of you achieving your goals will increase hugely.

Act as if

We all want bang for our buck. I understand the importance of effectively getting a result in the shortest period of time. I want to take one thing that's really an issue and, within a single session, be able to create some real change.

People ask me, 'How do you make changes really quickly?'

If I have to make a difference in someone fast, the first thing I do is change their physiology. If someone tells me they lack confidence, I tell them to act as if they have all the confidence in the world. The brain decides that we need to be congruent with whatever we verbalise, so if we sound like we're confident, our brains will act accordingly.

If you've convinced yourself you can't do something, and you decide to just go through the motions, you've got no chance of proving that you can do it. If you give yourself that elbow room to be fearless with it and not worry about the outcome but just be present, that improves probability.

If you're constantly out there improving probability because you're not limiting yourself, and you're seeing challenge through a different lens, what are the possibilities? They're huge!

For instance, say you're in a situation at work where you're not feeling confident about presenting in front of people and you're anxious about it. The reality is that you're still responsible for having to act in that moment. To support yourself to put forward the best version of yourself – recognising that you're anxious and you don't know if you're good at it – first, you need to change your physiology and work on your breathing. Then you need to act as if you already have what you need to succeed.

When I run this exercise, I say, 'If you were confident right now and you knew they would absolutely love everything you've got to say, what would you be thinking and feeling?'

Immediately, that unlocks something. The person will start running through exactly what they would say and how they would feel. That's usually followed by a moment of realisation that their limitations were self-imposed, for no reason.

'Act as if'. Once you get over the fear of failure, you'll realise how silly it was.

I'm a prime example of that. I had a limited lens around education. As I started to take responsibility for what I needed to learn, and started to learn *how* to learn, it became something I was excited about. My model of the world went from quite small to huge, and it continues to constantly expand. That's really living life!

When you know that you're good at something you previously thought you couldn't do, it feels so good; it's incredibly fulfilling.

Dissociate and borrow resources

When it comes to 'act as if', the average person doesn't have to be a superman or superwoman, and they might not need an alter ego, but they can still use the same resources if they need to. This is a process I call dissociating – imagining you're someone else for a period of time – and borrowing resources.

Choose someone who you admire, someone who is an expert in the field that you're working within. There are no rules as to who you choose, it's more about you getting out of your own way to improve the probability of a series of outcomes that you can be excited about. By letting go of our limiting beliefs and our identity, through a visual process, we can act as if we're someone else.

The beauty of doing this lies in the fact that it blocks potential contamination through perception. When we go through a process and think *I'm acting now*, we don't have to rely on the thinking process. We're just pretending.

Sometimes the biggest problem we have is sabotaging ourself through our own perceptions, so we spend more time convincing ourselves that we can't do something than making a real attempt. Sometimes we make the mistake of heading to the opposite end of the spectrum and we try too hard.

The thought process behind dissociating and borrowing resources is, *Hey, you know what? It's not me, so I can leave reality behind, and for a moment, I can pretend.*

In the pretending, believe it or not, because you're not having contaminating thoughts, you will realise that you have greater opportunities than you thought and the possibility of what you can achieve increases. While you're there, you also have a high probability of realising that you've been bullshitting yourself all along, and you actually *are* good at the thing you thought you couldn't do.

A great example of this process is a client of mine who called me up and said she needed to see me because she had an important game of golf coming up. When she called, I happened to be at the golf club as well. I went and found her, and the first thing she said to me was, 'I can't play bunker shots, David.'

I threw some balls in a bunker and said, 'Show me.'

Sure enough, she was terrible. We're predictive, right? She'd verbalised it, so therefore she had to prove it. People do this all the time.

I said, 'We're going to play a little game. I know you're interested in conquering this.'

She said, 'But it'll take me hours …' (Excuse.)

I said, 'No, it won't. You watch this.'

I told her she needed to disassociate and borrow resources, then 'act as if'.

I wanted her to verbalise in a way that showed she was consciously aware of how to set up for a shot. That would mean she could hold herself to account to ensure that both her intentions and her attention were congruent with desired outcomes

'There's no one here, so let's have some fun with it.'

She said OK, so I suggested a little bit of roleplay. I asked her who her favourite golfer was.

'Annika Sörenstam.'

'Bear with me and let's play a game. Let's just pretend you're Annika and you're running a seminar for a whole lot of ladies on how to hit a ball. I want you to talk me through what you'd tell them.'

She started out talking quite quietly.

I said, 'Speak up! You've got a whole lot of women here listening to what you have to say.' Then I asked her to explain the key things required to set up a shot. I threw a ball into the bunker.

'One of the key things is setting up your feet and digging them in, as that allows the club …' and off she went.

I asked her to show me.

She went and hit the ball out of the bunker.

I said, 'OK, what would you do if you wanted to come out softer?'

'You adjust accordingly and get your body position right …' Then she looked up, laughed and said, 'What the hell have you done to me?'

'I haven't done anything. You did it!'

She'd got out there and found she had no more excuses. Her brain had gone, 'We've got two options here. We can go back to the old programme, or we can use the new one. This new one makes us feel good so let's commit to that.'

I still get the odd text from her now and then: 'Dave, I

had a good game. I was in the bunker on the 12th. You'd be proud of me! I was Annika!'

Who's going to know that she was being Annika? Absolutely no one. Nobody's going to come up and say, 'You're cheating because you're being Annika!'

That's the power of the alter ego.

Managing anxiety

Anyone who has really put some effort into something will have some level of anxiety. It shows that whatever you're putting your time and effort into means something to you.

What athlete doesn't get slightly anxious before an event? They all do. What I teach is how to start managing that anxiety as opposed to surrendering to it.

I still get anxious when I submit an essay. I'll hit submit then think, *Was that the right file I just uploaded?* I know that's my go-to because I made that mistake once and I got hammered for it.

What happens then is that you get sensitised to a specific moment, then because that emotional response is embedded into the memory, any time you come to a similar situation that becomes your frame of reference, so you have those associated feelings.

Part of the purpose of the ego is to protect us. It will take experiences and go, 'This is important and I want to do well,' and then the negative self-talk will kick in, as a misguided effort to prepare us in case something goes wrong. The brain is an amazing thing!

It's important to have the self-awareness to feel that feeling, then step back and have a conversation with yourself about where the anxiety is coming from, rather than climbing all the way into it.

I tell my clients, 'I don't want you to surrender to the emotions.' That emotional response doesn't necessarily mean that it's reality. Our brain lies to us.

The map is not the territory

Polish philosopher Alfred Korzybski coined the saying, 'The map is not the territory.' The 'map' is our understanding of reality – the 'territory' – which is an incredibly powerful idea. We have to appreciate that, as conscious beings, we don't have access to reality. When it comes to our programming, we can only process so much information at a conscious level – we need to use a map.

Maps are really useful for helping us get from A to B and for helping us to understand the geography of a place; however, a map doesn't show us the potholes on the road, the damage caused by a recent storm or the new building that has just gone up. A great example of this is the map of the London Underground system. The actual layout of the stations on the Underground differs hugely from the way they're shown on the map, which was designed for ease of use rather than as a direct representation of the network.

We can only deal with a couple of bytes of information at a conscious level, by which I mean in the sense of remembering and tasking. But the subconscious mind is constantly processing millions of bytes of information.

For instance, one of the most important modalities is visual. The light comes in through the eye and hits the retina, it's then processed. But the brain has a mechanism that helps us cope with all the information. It will:

- Delete
- Distort
- Generalise

Here's an example. If I said to you, 'I want you to tell me about the population of China,' there are two ways you're likely to respond. You'll either tell me the approximate number of people in China, or you'll tell me about the different ethnic groups that live in China. The last thing you're going to do is sit there and go through the alphabet, naming every person who lives in China.

You've chosen to generalise the information in order to answer my question. Is that generalisation a true representation of the population of China? No, it's not. But it's what our brain is capable of processing.

We also delete and distort information. The reason for that is that we couldn't cope with the entirety of reality. If we had to deal with everything thrown at us in its complete form, we'd be overwhelmed with sensory information. Instead, the brain has these mechanisms to help us cope so that we don't become overwhelmed. If it didn't, the information overload would turn our brains to soup. That filtering process is a positive thing in that it protects our conscious minds, but it can also be a negative thing.

The representation that we end up with is not necessarily the truth. Psychologically, because we're filtering so much information by deleting, distorting and generalising, there's no single, true representation of reality. Whether we like it or not, we don't have access to reality. Everything is filtered.

However, the brain can only filter what we feed it. In this way, it's a lot like a computer – when you feed it bad data, it will produce bad data, but when good stuff goes in, good stuff will come out. To ensure your brain is producing the good stuff, you need to be conscious and aware of what you're putting into it.

If your brain is going to delete, distort or generalise the information you feed it, then it's important to be able to ask yourself whether the original data is trustworthy and from a credible source. Similarly, you need to ask yourself whether that data has the potential to contaminate your thinking.

Remember, the quality of your life is directly related to the quality of the questions you ask yourself.

Perception is projection

One of the most magnificent things that exists is the eye. It's amazing how our eyes have evolved, but they never give us access to reality itself. We all have our interpretations of what reality is. If you're aware of that, you can start to understand the importance of the fact that we project what we perceive.

The mind works a bit like the interfaces of a computer. You see a file, then you delete it. That's kind of a representation of how the brain works.

If we went beyond that basic process of seeing and deleting a file into all the zeros and ones that create the code for every piece of data on our laptop or phone, we wouldn't be able to cope with what that all truly represented. We'd become overwhelmed. That's why we delete, distort and generalise.

We build up information over time and the brain uses that information to find shortcuts. The brain has to go, 'OK, what's my frame of reference? I see a round thing. What do I remember that from? I've seen it on a car. It must be a tyre.'

When it comes to framing, sometimes you've got to really challenge what the brain is telling you. This is about igniting your ability to think critically rather than letting our brains default to shortcuts that they've built up subconsciously over time. A good example of this is you might see someone walking along and notice that they've got a lot of tattoos. Social conditioning might then cause your brain to say, 'Watch out! That person has tattoos – they might be a criminal.'

Your behaviour towards that person will change based on that perception. Whereas, in reality, if you stopped to speak to that person, you might find that they're a softly spoken, highly educated professional.

I'm sure people look at me and make judgements about me based on nothing but how I look. I reckon a lot of them would be pretty surprised if they took the time to find out about the real me.

Our values and our memories also influence the way our brains filter things. Sometimes they have to be challenged too, but this has to be done in a respectful way. I know where I stand with my beliefs and values, and I know I'm able to protect myself and what I believe and value. At the same time, I have to be respectful of other people's models of the world.

Intentions and attention aligning

It's important that your intentions and attention align. When Clive, who was my original coach, said that to me, I thought, *That's really cool, but I don't know what it really means.*

I'm happy to admit that it's something that took me a while to truly understand.

You manifest and reinforce your world through your words. You might be saying one thing – your intention – while your brain is focused elsewhere – your attention.

One guy I spoke to said, 'I just lack confidence. It always stuffs me up when I start to–'

I interrupted him. 'Think about this. We've talked about our intentions and attention needing to align, right? What is it you want to do?'

'I want to run a marathon.'

'OK, so that's your intention. Where is your attention?'

'What do you mean by that?'

'Your representation and the beliefs you hold. Tell me again what your intention is.'

'I want to do a marathon, but I'm a shit runner.'

'I'm going to stop you there, mate. Did you hear what I just said about representation? How does you saying you're a shit runner align with that goal?'

We went through the same conversation several times. Eventually, I stopped the conversation because I felt like I was working against myself. Sometimes, I find that even though I can see where I'm going with a client, I can tell that they don't quite get it. In those situations, I've got to remind myself to slow down. I'll pace myself and lead them until I see that 'aha!' moment. I can see it in their eyes when that happens. Those moments for me are magical.

You can't advance when there's resistance, so you've got to find other ways to move forward. The moment you get some resistance, you need to try to work out where that resistance comes from. Then, together, you can investigate it – 'How is this working for you?' – then they start to realise the impact that resistance is having on their lives. Once it's been acknowledged, it can be changed. Then you can continue to lead the process.

I get this resistance with a lot of athletes, but when their intentions and attention start to align it's like they've set themselves free.

Most people aren't even consciously aware of the negative self-talk that they're doing – either internally or externally. You can't stop it if you're not aware of it. For a lot of people, negative self-talk is on the periphery of their consciousness. They kind of know it's happening but they don't pay attention to it. Once we start getting an awareness of our representation – to ourselves and to others – we become conscious of it.

With this guy who said he wanted to run a marathon, the eureka moment wasn't so much about the goal-setting process as it was about him recognising that he was making it hard for himself. He said, 'It's like I was trying to sprint in mud!'

'Good luck with that, as you're not going to get far ...'

What are your intentions? Does your attention align with them? The foundation of that is behaviour. That's how we measure it, so that there's congruent behaviour where the language matches the intention matches the actions – and achieving this is a lifelong pursuit.

Think about your thinking process

In his 2011 book, *Thinking, Fast and Slow*, psychologist Daniel Kahneman put forward his theory that there are two main types of thinking process. System one is fast, unconscious and emotional, and it relies on stereotypes. System two is slower, conscious and logical, and it relies on effort being made.

Most people tend to think from system one – the fast system – which is more emotionally based, without any active thinking. System two, meanwhile, is all about slowing down, being critical and investing in what you're thinking about.

Given the fast-paced world we live in, where information is being served to you at every turn, it's not surprising that we resort to system-one thinking and don't put a lot of effort into critical thinking. Instead, people tend to go with the narrative that feels right for them.

If anything, I would want to encourage everyone to purposefully go out and seek intellectual conversation. Be selective about who you spend time with and be respectful of their different beliefs and ways of thinking, and you will find you can have a conversation without anyone getting offended.

That's why I have Breakfast of Champions every week. I sit down with people from different backgrounds with different ideas and ways of living. The discussion and banter are brilliant. We challenge each other, and I always leave feeling richer for having learned about other people's experiences, cultures and beliefs.

When you seek the best people, you'll find them. I've had some amazing moments. We all have these perceptions and we make judgements of people very quickly. I've had some of the most in-depth conversations with people who, if you observed them in society, you'd probably cross the road to avoid.

Part of it for me is, because of the way I was brought up, I can go through a fuller spectrum of culture. I've got friends who have been in prison through to people who are wealthy community leaders. Some people are limited by their perceptions of others. We tend to like people who are the most like us, which is understandable. But if we have our guard up, we'll never meet anyone who isn't just like us. We're all made so much richer by learning about other people's experiences.

Fear is your brain trying to protect you

Sometimes fear can serve us. If you're going to the beach, there are times when the sharks are feeding so it wouldn't be a good idea to go for a surf. The sharks don't care about your fear – they're out there living their life, doing their thing. We, as humans, need to be smart enough to know when to listen to fear and when not to.

There's something really powerful in being honest with yourself about where your fears are. Fears are worth investigating. Most people are so frightened of taking risks that they just don't do it. Sometimes the gift is in the redundancy – or whatever other hurdle you face – because in that moment you have to face up to the things you fear as you have no other option. The gift comes after the initial 'shit my pants' event, which is what most people spend their lives trying to avoid. Whatever's on the other side of that can be truly great.

When you do something new, there will always be that initial fear, but you've got to push through and get to the other side. It's a progressive thing. Once you start pushing the boundaries further and further, your nervous system will get used to it and you will stop feeling uncomfortable. That will help you to push past the fear.

I know for me, one of the biggest challenges was the influence of people around me. When I was 22 and wanting to create the business I have now, people around me told me they thought I was nuts. I didn't listen. I dared to design my life, and I'm proud of that.

If you want to walk on water, first you've got to step out of the boat. I was prepared to take that risk. With that risk,

I was prepared to take all responsibility. Did I have setbacks and did I struggle? Bloody oath, I did.

It's when you're in that place of vulnerability and struggle that it's easy for other people to say, 'See, I told you so!' Sometimes that comes from a misguided desire to protect, but a lot of people don't like to see anyone else exceed what they've done themselves.

That's where you need a clear vision, resilience and a strong self-image to persevere. Most people who might be interested in making big change give up the moment they start failing. Instead of giving up, they should have reframed that failure to serve them.

On your journey to fulfilment, you have to go through pain and you need to go through failure. You need to go through these things because they test your resolve.

Action is the true measure of intelligence

Once you acknowledge and investigate your fears, then you can come up with a strategy to overcome them. Perhaps you want to complete a marathon and you don't know if you've got the mental fortitude to do it. What's the strategy for you to build that mental edge?

A lot of mental fortitude comes from time under tension, which involves facing up to fear and taking action. Say you know that the marathon you want to do is 42.2km. Right now, you might be able to run 2km. How many weeks do you have before the marathon? You don't need to go out and run 42km tomorrow. Instead, it's a case of divide and conquer, then put together a plan. Work out how much faster or further you want to be able to go, week on week, and gradually you'll build that time under tension, and with it your mental strength and self-belief that you can run a marathon.

Taking action through facing the things that we fear is powerful. Once you start overcoming fear, your model of the world will change and expand dramatically.

Mind your language

The other thing that is important in this process is using supportive language. We're almost unconscious of when we express things, but the mind pays attention and starts to develop belief systems around what's being represented. If we're aware of those things, we can change the language and then we can start accelerating.

If you catch yourself saying, 'I always do this,' change it to 'I do everything I can to reach my goal.'

'It's so hard,' to 'It's so worthwhile.'

'I really would like to, but …' to 'I really would like to, so …' (When you use the word 'but', your brain negates everything that is said before it.)

The realisation of those weaknesses can then feed into the construction of your affirmations.

'I'm a do-it-now person.'

'It's easy for me to run a marathon.'

Get comfortable being alone

I think in today's world, the biggest thing a lot of people fear is being alone. If you can spend time alone in honest reflection and deep discovery, seeking the things you fear, that is the biggest gift.

As Jung said, 'Where your fear is, there is your task.'

We get bombarded with a lot of societal noise every day. There's something really nice in having a little isolation and a little quiet time. I'm not suggesting going bush for months (although if that's your thing, go for it!), but there's no reason why you can't have some quiet time for yourself to reflect and plan. I think one of the most beautiful things you can do is have time alone, but most people, especially the ones who are still in the camel phase of Nietzsche's metamorphosis, seem to be scared of that because when they're alone, they have to acknowledge and listen to the lion talk – and it will be roaring. For them, the thought of spending hours alone in silence can be quite overwhelming.

If you struggle to spend quiet time alone, try approaching it as if it's a new skill you need to learn. Set time aside to practise it and make it a goal to slowly build the amount of time you spend in quiet contemplation. I think it's important to do this somewhere comfortable and, if possible, outdoors.

If you struggle to slow your mind, try doing the four-five-slow breathing exercise (page 156), then do a scan down your body, relaxing each set of muscles as you go. If you struggle with feeling like you should be doing something else, remind yourself that it's OK to be still and relax.

Spending time alone allows you to quietly investigate, ask questions, self-analyse and reassess. It also allows you to check in on your goals and, if necessary, set new ones.

People are constantly comparing themselves to others. Nietzsche talked about how we start to resent those who are successful. I say, 'Define success.' For each of us it will mean something different.

Reframe failure

On one test I did, I got a mark that I wasn't happy with. Instead of getting upset, I made a conscious effort to reframe my response. I decided to find out what I could have done differently in order to achieve a different result. It was then that I realised I'd misread the assignment.

I could have gone down the blame route by saying the test had been poorly designed, but that was too easy. Instead,

I used the experience as a lesson to read assignments more closely in the future.

When you really, truly own things that happen, that is a gift in and of itself, regardless of the outcome. If you seek to blame instead, you're really missing out on the lessons you could be learning.

I'm really committed to doing the best that I can with my study. That doesn't guarantee me A-pluses, but I know that I'm doing all that I can by holding myself to a high level of accountability. That's reflected in my behaviour when it comes to studying. I'm motivated by the promise I've made to be truly congruent. I can't expect any of my clients to commit themselves fully to the study process if I won't do that myself.

Did you do everything you could?

I have a pet hate – people who say, 'I gave it 110 per cent.'

You got a bad grade and you're going to now work really hard to convince yourself that you gave it your all. I think that's a cop-out. I'd rather see you constantly challenging yourself to see how you could have done better. How can I improve? How do I consistently pursue self-accountability to the point that I'm never quite satisfied?

If you're accountable to yourself, when you work as hard as you can and you get 60 per cent for an exam, chances are you'll be happy with that because you know the levels of expectation you've put on yourself.

You could surrender to the statement, 'I'm not expecting to do well.' Instead, I encourage you to choose to think about the bigger picture and the goal: 'I want to be the best version of myself.' In that case, I would have an override mechanism that changes the wording to, 'OK, because there's no expectations, let's see what I can do.' That's all about having the mindset of seeking to be the best version of yourself.

It's a bit like weight training. There are days when I know I'm absolutely knackered, but I'll still push myself – just in different ways. I'll adjust accordingly. I'm not going to go, 'I'm feeling knackered, so let's just do a little bit.' That's too easy. People go back to that easy default too often.

On those days, maybe it's an opportunity to push yourself to see just what you can achieve. Maybe it's an opportunity to have some sort of breakthrough.

Recently, I was training and I was tired. I just did my normal sets, then I thought, *I'm going to go lighter and I'm going to do sets of twenty instead of sets of eight.*

It's understanding the importance of being flexible and mindful, but at the same time still holding a slightly higher level of expectation and self-accountability.

The gift is in the feedback

What is it that allows someone to take negative feedback and not become a victim to it, but rather use it as motivation? That's one of the most powerful things you can do. A lot of people, when they get negative feedback or they fail at something, very quickly go to blame, excuse and denial, saying things like, 'That's not fair!'

I don't agree with that. I'm prepared to take things on the chin. I'm not going to challenge everything. If I get negative feedback on a university assignment, I will assume that a professor, who is truly committed to the integrity of their subject, is not going to say something vindictive to me just to piss me off.

Feedback should be something that helps guide you through life, but so often we're dismissive of honest feedback. Instead of taking it on board, we go, 'Poor me! I was deserving. I worked hard.' Working hard should be a non-negotiable! It should be required.

Instead of creating a victim story, take on board the fact that you failed and learn from it.

I've failed some of the tests and exams that I've had as part of my degree, and I've had a series of papers to write for one subject where my work was not up to scratch. You know what? I'm thankful for that because it slapped me. I read the feedback and the lecturer pointed out that my construction was the issue. That was a real gift to me. I could have sat there and said, 'That's not fair!' but I could see that it was honest and it was helpful for me in the future.

We shouldn't be expected to compromise or tiptoe about in case someone thinks what we're saying isn't fair.

There also needs to be a certain level of critical thinking when it comes to taking feedback from people. Especially in the online space, it seems to be that everyone's an expert today. This is where you've got to be careful in selecting your sources of feedback. More importantly, even before you totally commit to the source, make sure you investigate potential bias from their perspective.

If I'm getting feedback from a professor, it's valid. They're qualified to be making the comment. If I'm getting feedback from a mate in the pub, who's got no idea, it's unlikely to be valid, so I won't take it on board.

Seek to be the best version of yourself

Happiness is part of the goal, but not the be all and end all. In order to appreciate happiness, you have to have a frame of reference. It's like dark and light – you can't have one without its opposite. Ideally, what we want is to spend most of our time in light.

This is where the existentialist in me comes out. We have two options – we can go into nihilism and embrace the nothingness, or we can seek to be the best version of ourselves. Nihilism isn't an option as far as I'm concerned. Sartre and Camus ask questions like, 'What's the point of life, as it's absurd?' I say life *is* absurd.

As human beings we have this stupid, unrealistic expectation that life should be ideal. The reality is, we're here. Heidegger talked about the fact that we're thrown into this world, so we find ourselves here in a time that is not of our choosing. We have to find the best way to exist in our own situation. Ideally, for all of us while we're here, we should be making the most of what we've got. We can take responsibility for finding as much happiness as possible, while also accepting that it ain't going to be a free ride.

Now let's talk about determinism and how we can live within a determined world. As Daniel Dennett described it, we have elbow room for free will. Some neuroscientists might argue the point, but I believe that we have free will. We, as agents, have the ability to reframe things, to make better decisions, and to live life by design rather than default.

A lot of people lose sight of all the good there is in the world. Instead, they choose to focus on their anxiety and the negative things in their lives. If you can navigate your way around it, if you can endure it, if you can be resilient enough, then you can – for the majority of your time – seek happiness and purpose in your life.

Chapter 9

HAVE THE BEST OF INTENTIONS, BUT LET GO OF THE OUTCOME

Career-defining events and decisions

In this chapter, I'm going to take you step by step through a high-stakes event, what you might be feeling, the obstacles you might encounter and the techniques you can utilise to access the winning mindset. I'll mostly be discussing this in a high-performance sporting context, but the same mentality applies to any scenario where you are under pressure and need to perform at the top of your personal game.

Immediately before an event

By definition, high-performance athletes compete in highly charged events at which the stakes can be very high for them.

For some, the hype and excitement of event day charges them up, while others can find it intimidating.

Changing the channel

One night, I got a phone call from a swimmer who was at a big meet in Australia. She told me she hadn't done that well in her heats. I acknowledged what had happened, but these were secondary events for her and she should have seen them as a warm-up.

I said, 'Right now, can you change what has happened?'

'No. It's done.'

'You're going into your big event tomorrow, and we've discussed this – your last event, your last swim does not define you. But, right now, you're allowing it to define you. You're taking that energy into your favourite event tomorrow. How does that serve you? What are you going to do about it?'

She was quiet.

'So, what can you do right now to change that channel?'

'Well, it wasn't my key event.'

'No. It wasn't. What else?'

'I actually had two PBs coming into this comp, so I'm on track to put forward a really good time.'

'Fantastic! What else can we add? Let's build this cake. Put as many flavours in there as possible!'

'This is the best prepared I've ever been for this event!'

It changed her state of mind – and she went out and achieved a PB. In reflection afterwards, I said to her, 'What is the story about the story?'

She said, 'The story is I was telling myself a story that wasn't serving me, so when I change the story, I can change the outcome.'

The freak-out phone call

Sometimes before events, I get phone calls from athletes who are freaking out a bit. I like that they call me even though they know I'm not going to go, 'Right, here's what we'll do about it …' or, 'I know how you feel. It's awful.' They know I'm not about handing them a solution or giving them meaningless sympathy so that they feel better in the moment, because that doesn't help them in the long-term.

What's the worst thing you can say to someone when they're freaking out? 'Calm down.'

'Thank you! I never thought of that! You're brilliant. Good on you, Freud!'

I can understand that there's pressure, and I can understand that I'm the person who they contact, but I'm not here to rescue them. That's why my initial question is always, 'What can you do right now to put you on track to put forward the best possible version of you right now?'

What's interesting is I have them start to think and the initial answer will always be, 'Ohh, I don't know!'

My reply is always, 'Well, how does that help? How does that language help you?'

'You're right.'

'So what can you do?'

'I can change my language.' 'I can change my state.' 'I can change the movie in my head.'

All of a sudden, I see them regurgitating my Nietheisms!

'OK, so what are we doing tomorrow?'

'Oh, mate, all I can do is bring forth the very best version of me, so I'm going to make sure everything's in alignment.'

Use the alter ego

Don't worry about the outcome. Concentrate on the immediate, the present, and – if need be – use that alter ego. That's why the alter ego is so powerful.

One of the swimmers I work with is very introverted. She's also someone who is very caring, aware of others, empathetic and nurturing. Unfortunately, there's a time for empathy and there's a time for competition.

I've had heaps of clients embrace the alter ego. It's something they can go to every single time to help them change their physiology and perception. I could spend ages working on the self, but sometimes I have to come up with something that can work fast because the event's tomorrow.

We were talking about this and I said, 'So, what's the alter ego? What's the absolute opposite of you?'

Straight away, she said, 'I just see a shark.'

'What happens when you think of a shark? Does a shark give a shit what others think?'

'No way!'

'What does a shark focus on?'

'Its prey.'

'OK, what else?'

'It's magnificent in the water!'

The key thing here was the attitude. We wanted it to be almost predatory, almost primal, mean and selfish, egotistical even – the complete opposite of her. She used to come out, get on the blocks and be comparing herself to other swimmers. The day after that phone call, she went out and embodied those things about the shark that made her fearless, and she swam a beautiful race.

The day of the event

Leave your expectations behind

I believe in the law of attraction, so it's important to be clear on what you want. One of the formulas that really reinforces that is BICE. This formula was developed by American hypnotherapy pioneer Charles Tebbetts.

Belief
+
Imagination
+
Conviction
+
Expectation
=
Results

An undoubtable belief in yourself and your ability will allow you to envisage positive results and desired outcomes. Most athletes will have imagined these moments hundreds – if not thousands – of times in their mind. They've also had the conviction to behave in a way that's congruent with achieving the results they desire. That leaves us with expectation.

Understanding how to work with expectations is the important thing in avoiding anxiety. Expectations are important in the application of the structures of practice, recovery, et cetera. Why? Because they hold you to account to give your commitment. However, the most important thing is to ensure that expectations are left in the changing room when you go to an event. Never take expectations to an event.

Why? Because they can lead you to make the mistake of trying too hard. When you combine that anxiety with the expectation of wanting to perform well, most likely it will lead to disappointment.

I know that this seems counterproductive, but the idea is to go out there and act like you don't give a toss. I'm pretty sure if I told an Olympic swimmer that, they'd look at me and say, 'Are you serious? It's an Olympic final!' But if you've done the work and you've got an undoubtable belief in yourself, you don't need to take those expectations with you.

I worked with a young Olympian cyclist who was constantly stressed out because of the expectations she had of herself. We've worked on this together. She told me, 'There's something beautiful in going to a race and being clear on intent, but not giving a toss about the outcome. I wasn't getting overwhelmed. I wasn't getting myself wound up at all. But I had the ability to be clear-headed and mindful.'

The four pillars of performance

Your brain has a primary directive, which is to protect you. In order to achieve things we once didn't think possible, we have to condition the brain. That happens when we start creating belief systems. We also have to start training the body and the mind. There's no difference between a surfer, a long-distance swimmer or someone who's going under a 300kg squat. The process for each of them is the same. It requires progressive time under tension.

I talk about the four pillars of performance: the physical, the mental, the technical and the tactical.

Each of those things needs to be worked on. They are the pillars that uphold performance. However, that absolutely changes on the day of competition. You cannot get physically stronger seconds before a race, so physical disappears. You're not going to change your technique 30 seconds before an event, so technical disappears. You're left with mental and tactical.

Most athletes will have some tactics they apply in preparation for an event. However, you can have the best tactics in the world, but if you don't have belief to support them, those tactics are redundant. If you don't believe those tactics are going to work because you don't believe you're that good, they're no use to you.

Ultimately, it comes down to the mental. That is the most important of all the pillars.

For athletes, anxiety doesn't serve them in an event itself. For an event, ideally you should be calm and focused, but it's understandable that there may be anxiety in those moments.

For an MMA fighter, when you're being wrapped up you're probably thinking that in about half an hour you're going to be putting your life on the line. Anxiety in that situation is entirely understandable.

Changing perspective can be useful here. For example, imagine going back in time to the First World War. You're an 18-year-old in uniform, you're in the trenches. The bombardment's finished and everything is quiet. You're waiting for that whistle to tell you it's time to go over the top. If you took a moment to think about that, you could use that as fuel to really get some perspective on your own life.

Reframing anxiety

It's important to be realistic about the requirement, but in order to provide a foundation where you can increase the probability and potential of performance, reducing stress and anxiety is vital. The power of reframing is important here. It's still a razor's edge, and it's very important that we get this balance.

When I'm working with athletes who are concerned about being anxious on event day, I ask them what the signs of being anxious are.

'I get the shakes, there's a lot of noise in my head, and I feel sick in the stomach.'

The fact they perceive that as anxiety contaminates the probability of them succeeding, because they're aware of the fact that they're anxious. As humans, we're conscious beings, so we're aware of how we're responding in the moment. So we can mess ourselves up.

I'll say, 'I want to ask you this – have you ever been on a rollercoaster? Did you enjoy it?'

'It was awesome!'

'OK, so before you got on there, did you get the shakes?'

'Yeah!'

'Was there a lot of noise?'

'Yeah!'

'Was it fun?'

'YEAH!'

When it comes to learning to reframe things to serve you, let's change, 'I'm feeling anxious' to 'I'm feeling excited.' By reframing it like that, it changes your internal representation.

You're most likely to put forward a better performance when you're excited about something, as opposed to when you're anxious about it – even though the signs for the two states are very similar. Fundamentally, what I want is to help people make better choices. To do that, they need to ask, 'How do I change this lens?'

After the event

Having achieved the goal

While achieving a goal that they've set for themselves – like winning a championship or a medal – is something that all athletes will celebrate and be justly proud of, it's what happens after that which they might not have considered. Something I often have to work through with my athletes is what happens when they attain that goal. Then what?

If you train them correctly, they're almost automatically looking towards acknowledging that they're now onto the next part of their journey. Those who do that are able to apply the principles they've learned in order to set goals in different areas of their lives.

Other athletes can go into a state of depression because they know they've achieved something, but they haven't developed that ability to focus on the continuation of their journey. I encourage them to understand their lives from a broader and bigger perspective. You're not just defined by one rugby game, one golf game, or one fight. Life is so much bigger than that.

That experience further underlines the importance of setting goals that are unrealistic and a little scary. We're here for a limited amount of time, so let's extract as much living as we possibly can while we're here. I truly believe that if everyone had that attitude, the world would be a better place.

Having failed to achieve the goal

Most high-performance athletes are never satisfied. Never. They're always going, 'I could have done that better,' or, 'I could have focused more on that.'

People will say, 'Oh, they're being overly critical.'

But sometimes they do it from a different framing. They get excited about learning and improving. They'll take it on the chin. They won't sit there and go, 'Oh, but I tried so hard …'

When clients come to me, they have their initial goals. The underlying philosophy of success and failure I try to impart to them is to have the best of intentions, but let go of the outcome. Part of my process involves educating clients that just because they've trained hard doesn't necessarily mean they're going to attain their goals.

Some people have an unrealistic expectation that, if they're training hard, they'll smash their goals. Training hard can only improve the probability of the outcome. No one can guarantee anything – but that doesn't mean there's no point and you might as well quit. You can certainly improve the possibility and probability of attaining what you want.

There are also some people who have a projection of the best version of themself that is very tied in with certain goals. Failure to achieve those goals hits these people hard. Instead of identifying with the achievement of goals, they should tie the concept of being the best person they can be into the process.

Going back to the underlying philosophy, you start to understand the importance of how you frame up failure. We tend to rely on the physiological feedback – how it feels to fail – and that's not the best representation.

I've got a little saying that applies to failure: 'Pain means new life.' When you sense failure, it's painful. Fundamentally, human beings will do anything to avoid pain. Generally, what happens is we will then start to make excuses. If you fail at something, what's your immediate response? Few people say, 'I'm going to put my hand up and take responsibility for that.' Instead, they'll say, 'But I've trained so hard …'

Really? Define 'hard'.

'I could have done better but I had a couple of niggles that week …'

The reality is the universe doesn't give a fuck about your niggles, and it certainly doesn't give a toss about excuses or who you blame. Ultimately, true freedom comes from a place of taking responsibility. If it's going to be, it's up to me.

At the end of their career

One of the biggest career-defining decisions an athlete will ever make is when to retire. This career transition is often made even more difficult when the decision is taken out of the athlete's hands. While this process is often scary, it doesn't have to be overwhelming. Here I'll introduce some strategies to help make life-changing choices. These are as applicable outside the sporting arena as they are within it.

I've been involved in working with athletes through the stage of their career when they are preparing to exit. Sometimes, that involves helping them understand that, emotionally, it can be traumatic. Part of their identity is tied up in what they do, and that's being ripped away. They have to go through the whole process of establishing a new identity.

There can be several different things going through their minds. One is how they feel about the fact that their identity has been compromised. Then they have this process of guilt, where they feel like they're letting down their team, themselves and all the people who have been supporting them for years. How they navigate through that and get some perspective is important. It's about going back to their priorities.

We work through strategies they can put in place for their future, and we discuss possibilities for upskilling and education. I have seen many of my clients go on to work behind the scenes in sport, or become TV presenters, commentators, coaches and mentors.

One of the athletes I work with sustained some severe injuries, which required him to get serious surgery. He came to see me upset because he felt guilty that he was letting his team down. I reminded him that his overall health was what was important, and we talked about the importance of thinking about life beyond professional sport.

Through our conversation, I was able to help him reframe the changes that were coming his way. By helping shift his perspective from doom and gloom to feeling excited about the wonderful experiences that lay on the other side of sport, he was able to let go of the expectations he'd put on himself. He was also able to reframe his injury to see it as a sign of just how committed he had been to his sport, and to embrace the potential opportunities that lay ahead.

As he processed all of this, I could see that he was getting ready to dump all that guilt and to release himself from it. His physiology changed as he shifted from feeling bad about letting his team down to being excited about what the future held for him.

Hanging up your boots can be really challenging. Ideally, during your time in the sport – or job or whatever field you're in – you will develop a support network and work on your potential exit strategy before it's thrust upon you.

Sometimes that exit strategy can be presented in an untimely way and is premature. That's a significant thing for athletes to go through, but it doesn't have to be the end of the world.

When you've built a strong self-image, it allows you to be consciously aware of how you frame things up. It's totally understandable to go through an emotional rollercoaster ride of feelings. The important thing is how quickly and how effectively you move on in life, otherwise it can really start to contaminate your mindset.

That's why I think it's important to plan for a change of career before you're in the middle of one.

If you've got some sort of exit strategy, those things won't come as such a shock.

I worked with Kiwi boxer Alexis Pritchard and helped her prepare for the 2018 Commonwealth Games, where she won a bronze medal. We worked on a few different things during our sessions including her personal definition of success, giving herself permission to be a great athlete, and creating an alter ego that would help her step into the assertiveness she required in order to dominate in the ring.

As I was working with her, we knew that she was probably coming towards the end of her career, so we started developing a future plan.

She'd already qualified as a physio, but she told me she was passionate about getting into coaching. I was running a seminar at a girls' college, so I invited her to come along to spend some time talking to the girls. That gave her a sense of it, and she loved it. She's gone on from there and she's doing a fantastic job working with athletes at all levels and doing a lot of mentoring, which I reckon is really cool. She is also part of New Zealand's Olympic Games leadership team, where she specialises in nurturing the team culture and laying a caring foundation for high-performance athletes, so they can go out on the world stage to perform. What a beautiful way for her to use her experience and knowledge to improve things for others.

High-performance athletes are, generally, very self-motivated, so once they're given a task, they'll get right into it. Through their curiosity they'll start identifying some core things that excite them. Take, for example, Tracy Lambrechs, the weightlifter I worked with. She's using her experience in the sport to assist with the work she now does for Drug Free Sport New Zealand, travelling around, educating people – and she is loving it.

PROFILE

On his own terms

Alex Pledger

Basketballer

- Tall Blacks debut 2008
- NZNBL MVP 2011
- NBL championship winner New Zealand Breakers 2011, 2012, 2013, 2015
- Bronze medal winner, Commonwealth Games 2018
- NZBL championship winner, Waikato Pistons 2009, Auckland Pirates 2012, Southland Sharks 2018
- No 35 retired by Southland Sharks, 2023

A prime example of a sportsperson who has had to make some big calls sooner than perhaps he would have liked is Alex 'Chief' Pledger, the former Tall Blacks and Breakers centre, who was still playing professional basketball when he was diagnosed with colorectal cancer in 2021.

At the time, he was playing for the Southland Sharks, and doctors said that they thought he'd already been battling the disease for some years.

I worked with Chief when he was part of the New Zealand Breakers team that won the NBL in 2015. I'll never forget that beautiful buzzer-beating three-pointer by Ekene Ibekwe, which sealed the win against the Cairns Taipans and won the championship at North Shore Events Centre. It was magnificent.

Alex is a quiet guy, a silent achiever. He's a gentle giant, and he has a huge heart for everyone he meets. When he played for the Breakers he never shied away from media and could often be seen having his photograph taken with young fans. He understood how much this meant to the youngsters who follow the game.

At our coaching sessions, Chief liked to lie down, so I was glad that my couch was long enough to cater for his 2.15m frame! We worked on building self-esteem and confidence. He took it all in and then went on to produce the goods on the court.

At the time of his diagnosis, he was extremely fit and playing fantastic basketball. It was a real shock for me when I got the call from his partner Bailee to tell me that Chief had cancer.

Alex and Bailee got married in 2021. I was honoured to be part of the wedding party when they exchanged vows at Gibbston Valley Estate near Queenstown. Chief had just finished his chemotherapy, but he was determined to see his beautiful wife walk down the aisle. There was not a dry eye in the house that day. Both Alex and Bailee had been through so many challenges to get to their special day, and it was beautiful to be there to support them both.

After three months' treatment – and just six weeks out from his last chemo session and his wedding – Alex returned to the court for the Southland Sharks for their final home game of the 2021 season. In September that same year, he announced that he was cancer-free.

Chief then went on to play most of the 2023 season for the Sharks, before announcing his retirement from the game in early July.

In an interview with Marc Hinton before his final game, Alex said: 'The uncertainty, being diagnosed away from home, then having to relocate in the middle of a pandemic, it was a very stressful, scary and difficult time. I feel like I've got a second chance at life. It might seem silly boiling it down to one word, but I'm just happy.'[5]

Despite what he'd been through, he was able to bow out on his own terms. As a mark of respect for everything he'd achieved with the team, the Sharks retired his number, 35, and at the end of his final game they raised his singlet up into the rafters of Southland Stadium.

In the spirit of giving back, Alex and his wife, Bailee, have gone on to become ambassadors for Bowel Cancer New Zealand.

Chapter 10

NURTURING SUCCESS

The winning mindset for parents and children

A lot of people out there have strong opinions about the role that sport should play in their kids' lives. I get asked a lot of questions about kids and sport – often when people find out that I worked with Lydia Ko when she was still very young. Here are my answers to some of the questions I get asked most often.

Individual versus team sport?

I think more attention needs to be paid to what motivates kids when it comes to sport. Not all kids will be into team sport and competing against other people – and that's OK. If, from the age of seven to about fourteen, kids are encouraged to try out as many sports as they want, they'll likely find the one/s that work for them.

Given the chance, they'll figure out if they're team players or if they prefer competing in individual sports. Along the way, they'll also learn a lot about interaction, building relationships and how to be coached.

What are your thoughts on rewards for participation?

I want to support kids to get involved in school sport. For the younger ones, it should be all about participating for the first few years. For them, playing sport should be fun and if getting an award helps them to enjoy it, that's all well and good.

Once they're older, though, the 'Everyone gets a prize!' mentality does them a disservice, as it's disempowering. It tells them that all they have to do in order to get recognition is show up. That's not how life works. In my view, sport is like a metaphor for life. We're doing kids a disservice if they're not prepared for how the world really is – that there are winners and losers.

By that age, they shouldn't need rewards for participation. By then, they should be playing sport because they love it and are motivated to get out there and do it. They also need to learn to accept the realities of competition, but they shouldn't be defined by the fact that they lost a game, a race or an event. Instead, we should be using that to empower them.

Winning isn't always about coming first. Sometimes it's just simply about conquering something that's sabotaged your potential.

The important question for them is, 'How do you develop the mindset of a winner? How can you reframe that so it helps you? What lessons can you learn from that experience?'

When should my kid specialise?

I think kids should be given an opportunity to investigate as many individual and team sports as possible in order to get a feel for them and for what they want to do. Trying out a multitude of sports also really helps with neurological development and motor skills. They'll slowly gravitate towards what they really enjoy.

The early teens is the time for most children to start specialising, if they decide that's what they want to do. However, that is not a blanket scenario. There are always going to be kids like Lydia who know from a very young age what they truly love doing. She was the one asking, she was the one pushing, she was the one who wanted to always be out there hitting just one more ball.

If your child just wants to do that day in, day out, they don't feel disempowered, they don't feel tired, they're not being dictated to, they want to self-govern and they want to push, then let them go for it.

Be aware, though, that kids like this are the exception rather than the rule, so if your children don't want to put that level of work in, then that's OK too – just let them get out there and investigate everything that interests them. The worst thing you can do is to push them so hard that they stop having fun and they quit sport altogether.

Only a few show a passion for their chosen sport early on, and you need to be able to identify that. If you have someone in their early school years who has a skill and they can be transitioned and committed to, by the time they're 18, they'll be outstanding. They could be world class.

The fundamental teaching of high performance is time under tension. A continuum of high performance, high commitment over a long, sustainable period of time leads to world-class results.

Are there any short cuts?

People who perform well consistently over a sustained period of time do it because they have a strong work ethic. They outperform everyone else because they outwork everyone else. There are no short cuts.

I talk about seven-year cycles, give or take a year or two. It takes a good seven years of hard work to become competent.

Then the next seven years are spent developing that in the world. The seven years after that are all gold. You've got to do the hard work. Anyone that says otherwise is full of it.

If kids don't start building some resilience and people aren't honest with them about what it takes, their chances are very low. This is somewhere we've got to be really careful, but honesty will set you free.

It's important that they get real about what the requirements are. The best way to really reinforce that with kids today, and with adults, is to tell the truth.

Can I use your goal-setting strategies with my kids?

Yes! Start by getting them to set small, achievable goals. Once they've developed the habit of setting goals, they'll learn the value of focused attention and hard work. This process will also help them to build confidence. Just remember to have the best of intentions, but to let go of the outcome.

I've sat with kids and their parents and said, 'Here's your homework. Everyone's going to create their own vision board and I want you, as a family, to sit down and present them to each other and share what that vision is.'

What a beautiful way to engage with your family! What a great way for parents to understand what's driving their kids. By making individual vision boards, you're teaching your child that everyone is accountable for their own life and goals, and that's really powerful.

If your child is having difficulty making decisions, try to avoid telling them what to do. Instead, refer them back to their board, and ask, 'When you think about the goals you set for yourself when making your vision board, what decision do you think you can make now?'

By doing this, you're making them accountable for their choices.

The feedback I get from parents who I've taken through this process has been, 'It's so much easier. My child is more self-motivated.'

In that process, you can make a promise that all you're going to ask about is what happens *today*. You're not going to hassle them about something that happened yesterday or worry them about what might happen next week. The subconscious works in the now, so this will help lessen their anxiety and will also make them more comfortable in opening up to talk to you about things that are happening in their lives.

When your kids have clear goals, they'll also have a certain level of curiosity, excitement and motivation.

Think about when you were a kid. How many times did your parents go, 'Get up! You've got school,' and you struggled to get out of bed by 7.30 am to catch the school bus in time. But what was it like on Christmas morning? What time did you get up then, about 5 am? Why? Because of the anticipation of something exciting happening.

We want to dial that down a little bit, because we can't have a nervous system like that of a kid on Christmas morning all the time, but imagine walking through life knowing where you are going and feeling a bit excited about it. If you can get your kids into that mindset, it will give them purpose. They'll know why they're doing what they're doing. Then that accountability and vision will allow them to make better decisions.

How serious should it be?

Despite having the best of loving intentions, some parents can lose sight of the role they should be playing in their children's lives. This can cause tension in the context of sport. By getting too involved in their kids' games, whether that's from the sidelines, as a caddy or as a coach, they can risk doing damage by taking away the essence of fun because they're so worried about the outcome.

They need to understand what their role is and also understand that failure and fun are both important parts of the process that help young children to learn. If parents aren't aware of this, their child can end up resenting the sport.

Your kids are going to fail. A lot of parents are so averse to that happening and so worried that it's going to damage their child that they try to prevent it from happening. To that I say that if they're having fun and they learn to reframe and take lessons from failure, they'll be much stronger, more resilient human beings.

Should I be concerned that my kid sometimes cries at sport?

People have to appreciate that young kids get emotional, they cry, they express themselves. When that happens, parents become concerned. However, they need to understand that their child's brain is still developing. The first part of the brain to be developed is the primal part, which is more emotionally based. Of course, their first course of action is to express themselves. Sure, the last thing I want a kid to be doing is throwing their clubs and having a hissy fit, so absolutely call them out on that. But it's OK for them to be upset.

This is even more problematic when there's a parent on the sideline who has been brought up to not show any emotion, so they don't know what to do with it.

I'm not afraid to show emotion and I will cry at significant moments. Sometimes when my athletes are competing, I'm so invested that it becomes too much for me and I can't watch! I get like that because I know the sacrifices they've made and what they've been through to get to where they are in life.

My child wants to quit. What should I do?

Sometimes I have to help younger athletes who are starting to get some success and suddenly find themselves thinking *Do I really want this?* Having had that thought, they feel trapped because coaches, friends and parents are so invested in their sport.

In that situation, dealing with other people's expectations can be very overwhelming for athletes. How do I help them deal with their anxiety? Sometimes it's about giving them a bit of elbow room or flexibility so they don't feel so trapped.

I might get a message from a parent going, 'You need to convince them that they need to commit to this.' That just doesn't sit right with me ethically. If I'm going to be a manipulator for the parents, then I shouldn't be doing this job. I have a reputation for keeping things real and being blunt and honest. That sometimes means that I need to have a conversation with Mum and Dad in order to clarify their roles.

'What is your role as a parent? It's to be unconditionally loving.' They get the loving parent bit, it's the unconditional part that some of them struggle with. Often that's because they're projecting their own conditions onto the child.

This might be a young teenager, who is still confused in life because they're going through a transition from dependency to independence, on top of all the biological changes they're experiencing. They feel like everything is being dumped on them at once and they're expected to perform at a high level.

They're starting to become independent thinkers and sometimes they realise, 'I've been doing this to appease Mum and Dad, and the passion's gone.'

The indicator for me will be a parent going, 'Oh my God, they're just not performing!' There's a number of different factors that can cause that, but as you investigate with a client the cause will become clear.

Spending time with people, I get a sense of them. With one client, I got a sense that things weren't right through a change in their physiology and a comment they made about an event that was coming up. I asked what was happening, and within 30 seconds this athlete was in tears. They told me that they were feeling overwhelmed by having to deal with other people's expectations of them.

It was important to help this individual navigate their way through how they were feeling. As humans, we want to move away from pain, so the easiest thing for them to do was quit. There were two things I saw that I needed to do: help give them perspective, then introduce some strategies before they started making decisions.

It's hard to get perspective when you're freaking out, so first we had a conversation about what was really happening. As a result, they realised that there were a lot of things they loved about their sport, and that they didn't want to lose sight of those things.

Second, I wanted to fold in the idea that this conflict itself was a beautiful thing, even though it might not feel like it. It was beautiful because it was challenging them and helping them build resilience. It was a reflection of life's challenges, which they would find a way to navigate through.

Having been in tears within 30 seconds of arriving, this person left saying, 'I feel like a weight's been lifted.'

It wasn't, 'I'm going to go and tell Mum and Dad I'm quitting.' It was, 'I'm going to start reframing this.'

Most parents really want the best for their kids. They may not be consciously aware of what they say and the pressure they can cause. I encouraged this athlete to have a conversation with their parents, which they did. From that conversation came the reassurance that they needed: 'No matter what, we still love you.'

That took the pressure off, and their performance started to improve.

How can we help our child's team to work together?

A guy I'd done a bit of work for asked me to go and have a chat with his son's rugby team, which was struggling a bit.

They were quite scattered and seemed a bit detached. They weren't working as a unit.

I decided to run an exercise that I call 'levitation'. Its purpose is to prove that when a team can focus their attention and work together efficiently with clear intentions, they can achieve outstanding results.

The exercise started with one of the bigger players sitting on a chair, with four smaller players standing around him – two on either side of the chair.

For the first part of the exercise, I ask the four standing players to each place their index and middle fingers under the knees and arms of the seated player, then to try to lift him out of his seat.

Of course, they'd been set up to fail, as I hadn't given them any clear instructions on how to do this effectively.

For the second part of the exercise, I added clear instructions to each player on their role and I made sure they focused their attention on what I was telling them to do.

Again, they placed their fingers in position, and they lifted the seated player off his chair and up over their shoulders.

How did they do this?

I gave them clear instructions and framed up what was going to happen. I then asked the four standing players to hold their hands over the seated player's head while ensuring that they didn't touch the top of his head or each other's hands.

The seated player said, 'I am as light as a feather' out loud four or five times. Then, on my command, the four standing players placed their fingers back into the positions under the seated player's knee and arms and lifted their teammate up above their shoulders. They realised the power of working together, and I think it helped them realise that they could do things they didn't think they could.

The parents were soon commenting on the change they'd seen in the team and in their kids. That's a real buzz for me.

Working with teams, the components still need to be broken down into individual responsibility, but that individual responsibility adds to the collective synergy of the team. If all members have that mindset, what you create is huge.

In that case, a large bowl of crystal-clear water represents the *team's* collective consciousness. Therefore, each individual's negative thoughts and actions can contaminate the *team's* collective consciousness.

Where can I find good role models for my kids?

Start by looking in the mirror. You model behaviours for your children. We're all a combination of all the things that made up the people who came before us. Children look for a variety of rolc models. Most importantly, it will be their parents who shape them in life. However, great role models will also be grandparents, caregivers, teachers and sports idols.

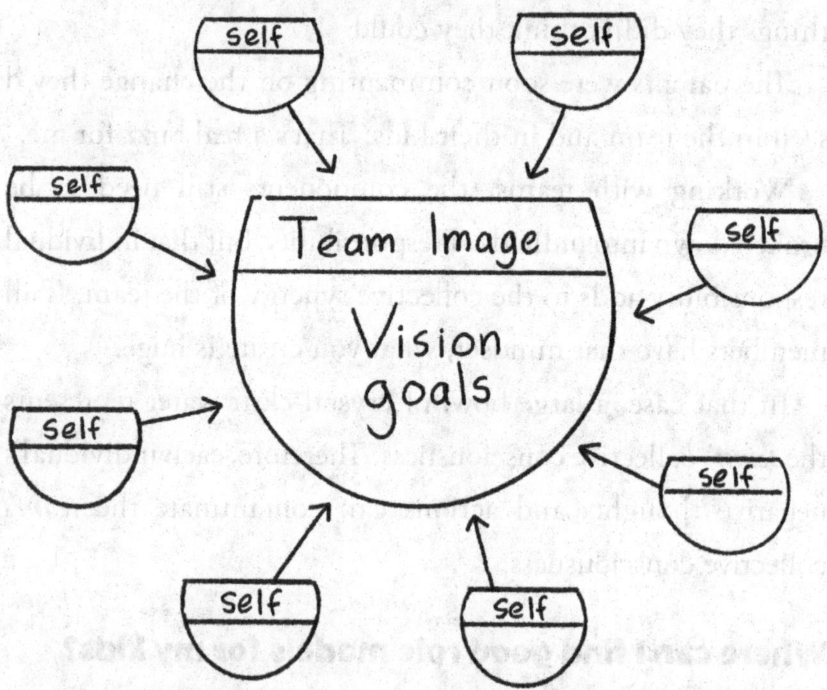
Each member brings the appropriate attitude each day
self
self
self
self
Team Image
Vision
goals
Self
self
Self
self
Each individual, by managing their self image, protects the collective

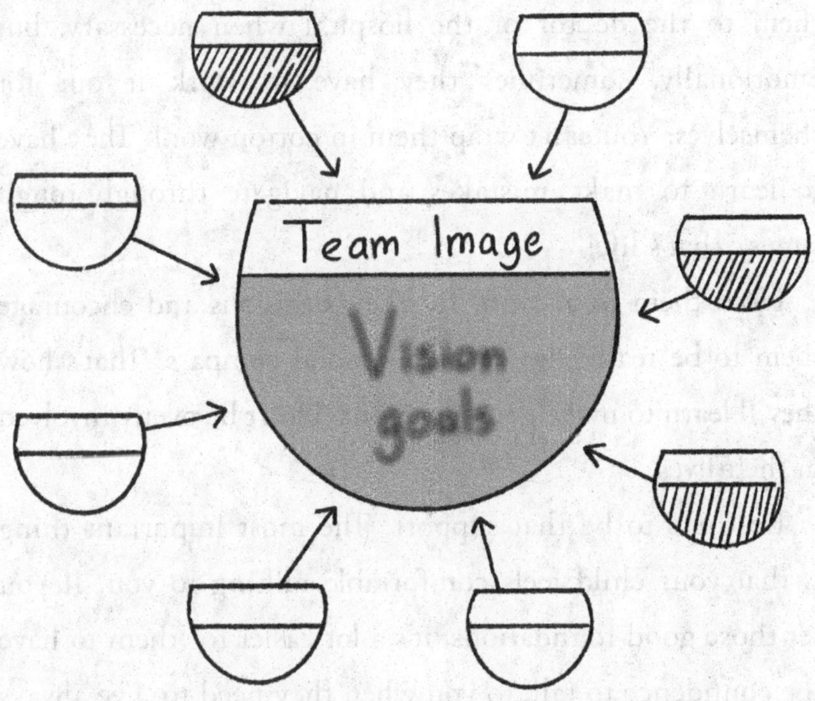
Contaminated team
loses its vision goals & focus
Team Image
Vision
goals

How involved in their lives should I be?

How many teenagers are very quick to manifest a story of how hard they've had it with their mum and dad? In the big scheme of things, they've probably got a phone and a computer, they're clothed, they're warm, they're educated and they're fed. A bit of perspective is required.

As a parent, you don't want to see your kids hurt or upset. In the physical sense, absolutely you want to take them to the doctor or the hospital when necessary, but emotionally, sometimes they have to work it out for themselves. You can't wrap them in cotton wool. They have to learn to make mistakes and navigate through tough times. That's life!

Hold them to account for their decisions and encourage them to be really clear on their moral compass. That's how they'll learn to make good decisions. Don't be overly involved in their lives.

Be there to be that support. The most important thing is that your child feels comfortable talking to you. If you set those good foundations, it's a lot easier for them to have the confidence to talk to you when they need to. I've always said to my kids, if ever you're in a situation where you feel uncomfortable, use me as excuse. 'Mate, I can't, my old man would kill me if I did that.'

It's inevitable that your children will go through tough times. Sometimes you need to give them a bit of support, but they have to work stuff out for themselves.

My child is being bullied. What should I do?

Bullying is a terrible thing. I've been through it physically and mentally. I don't know what sort of person I would have become if I hadn't been bullied; I wouldn't be the person I am today. Some people are so affected by bullying that they go down in a really negative way. I went in the other direction and became more resilient and determined. I still remember the day that I made the decision that put me on that path. I'm so proud of that.

Weirdly, I'm almost grateful for having been bullied, as I've become a better person because of it. Was I already at a certain level of resilience then that I could endure and reframe it in a way that served me? I don't know.

I'm interested in looking at how to take the concept and use the lessons I learned in a safer way, to build resilience. That requires good leadership, good coaching, good parenting, and being mindful of not falling into the victim's trap.

Kids internalise things that aren't theirs to own. 'Mum and Dad are fighting again – it must be my fault.'

The map is not the territory. If a kid's being bullied, they shouldn't be made responsible for the solution to the problem.

I'm coaching a young kid who is being bullied, and I'm helping him through it. There are a number of different things we've talked about. I'm not always the most politically correct person, but I certainly didn't say, 'Next time you see him, just punch him.'

I said, 'For all this fear and anxiety that have been created, I want you to think about this: success is the best revenge. What does that look like when you think of it?'

He said, 'Being on the podium and looking down at them.'

When he came second in his event, I said, 'How do you feel about it?'

He said he felt fantastic.

We reframe things to serve us.

The other thing you've got to appreciate, especially with kids, is that when they're thinking about their future, it's what's right in front of them. They're not thinking about when they're 30, 40 or 50. They're thinking about what's happening on the weekend or next week.

For this kid, I was able to give him something longer term to focus on, and it gave him some freedom. After the sessions I had with that young guy, I had a call from his mum. She said, 'Dave, I don't know what you've done, but we haven't heard anything more about the bullying.'

This is a guy who is becoming fearless and setting himself free by building resilience.

PROFILE

Tenacity and talent

Lydia Ko

Professional golfer

- 20 LPGA tour wins at time of writing
- 7 Ladies European tour wins at time of writing
- First LPGA tour event won 2012, at age 15
- Halberg Supreme Award winner 2013
- Named one of *Time* magazine's 100 most influential people in 2014
- Evian Championship winner 2015
- Youngest player (male or female) to reach number one on the World Golf Rankings at seventeen years, nine months and nine days of age, on 2 February 2015
- Appointed Member of New Zealand Order of Merit for services to golf in 2019

When I started seeing Lydia she was about nine or ten and when she sat on my couch her feet didn't touch the ground. We worked together for a good eight years. When she first came to see me, I asked her to make a vision board. She took to the task with much enthusiasm. While most kids who make vision boards cover them in stickers, medals and certificates that they've already won, Lydia wasn't having any of that.

At our next session, I could see how excited she was to share her vision board with me. She had cut out a picture from a *Golf Digest* magazine, showing Annika Sörenstam holding the Solheim Cup, then she'd popped a picture of her own head on top of Annika's body. That's how clear she was on that vision from the outset.

The blessing for her was that she was always enthusiastic, and that enthusiasm never wavered. There was a consistency, not just of behaviour, but of curiosity and energy and excitement for the things she needed to do with her training. She had found her passion and was committed to doing everything she could to achieve her goals.

Our sessions were always fun. I spent time with Lydia helping her to visualise playing at tournaments, playing shots and winning. From a young age, she was learning how to get the best out of her mind while in pursuit of being world number one.

Lydia took control and drove our sessions. She would debrief her games, then we would look at what had worked and what hadn't. Together, we'd find new strategies that would help her to become more aware of her thought processes both on and off the course.

I've often been asked about Lydia's success, and usually the questions turn to the role of her parents in her career.

Like a lot of parents whose kids are fully committed

to their chosen sport, Lydia's parents were extremely supportive of her. They saw that she was talented, but talent wasn't all she had. She had real tenacity. The true key to Lydia's success was one simple question she would ask frequently: 'Can I hit just one more?'

She was always the one asking the question – she was never told that she *had* to hit one more ball.

There's a little saying I like: 'What's done in the dark will shine in the light.' And that was Lydia to a T.

Her parents saw her passion and dedication, the hours spent on the golf course and at the driving range. Her mum would make her snacks and a packed lunch and off she would go. Lydia was so dedicated that she was given her own key to the driving range so she could lock up, as she was always the last to leave.

People who excel in life are prepared to work harder than everyone else. The sad thing is that other people will then be jealous and resentful of the people with a strong work ethic, of the people who are tenacious, of the people who put in that extra effort when they themselves aren't willing to do it.

By creating that narrative, you're giving yourself a reason to believe that not everyone can have the level of success that Lydia's had. You're just bringing it down and finding another reason you can't be like Lydia, why you can't have that winning mindset.

Chapter 11

BUILDING UP WINNERS

For coaches or people who want to become coaches

True wisdom comes to each of us when we realise how little we understand about life, ourselves, and the world around us.

—Socrates

Integrity is vital

I truly believe that the only true way to wealth – and we're not talking about money, we're talking about *wealth* – is to help others get what they want. When I can help my clients achieve what *they* want, I'm helping to create what *I* want. That's why it's fulfilling. By doing what you do well, you'll impact other people's lives in a positive way.

There's a huge amount of responsibility in dealing with people. One of my core values is integrity, in the sense of congruent coaching. It's important to be fully aware of what your strengths and weaknesses are. For me, when I recognise that a person needs deeper psychological help I'm quick to say, 'Listen, that's not really what I do and I will refer you on,' because that's the ethical thing to do.

The craft of coaching

Coaching for me is a craft. I'm really protective of it.

I know I harp on about congruence a bit, but that's because it's so important. A huge part of my development as a coach has been the struggle that I've been through. My coaching is a combination of what I've learned together with my life experience, which has given me a little bit of wisdom.

Knowledge and experience come together to make people good at what they do. Fundamentally, I am blessed with both. It comes down to craftsmanship and putting the hours in to learn that craft – and that's something that applies no matter what you want to achieve in life.

Developing any craft can only truly be done through time under tension. To make sure I achieved my coaching goals, I had to buckle down and concentrate.

For me, coaching is about having a passion for the people I work with and for what I can help them achieve. When I get asked about significant moments in my coaching career, I know people want big stories about title fights and celebrities, but I'll tell them a story about a bloke whose name they wouldn't even know getting a PB in the pool. That's as significant to me as any high-profile achievement.

There's something I really love about being in this office, talking to an individual one-on-one and helping them become the best version of themself. I'm so happy with what I'm doing. I love coming in here, sitting down and having incredible conversations with people.

My number-one value is freedom. I like that I can make my own decisions. I've designed my life the way I want it to be. I want to be able to reflect back on my life and think *I'm really proud of what I've done.*

Everyone starts somewhere – some of us don't give up

Commit to what you believe in, because there are a lot of false people out there who spend their lives worrying about what other people think. Don't buy into that same mentality. Don't be weak and compliant. Stand fast.

I've done this for 30 years. I am still evolving as a coach. What I do know is what I *don't* know, but I trust the fact that what I do makes a difference.

In the last 15 years, quite a few of my clients have been people who want to get into this industry. There are two reasons I help them. First, I'm concerned about the quality of some of the coaches out there. They read a book, do a two-week course and think they're God's gift to coaching. I want to protect the integrity of the industry by having coaches who are congruent. To do that, you need to hold yourself to account and continue your education to increase your understanding. I want them to model that from me.

Second, they're not my competition. That's the wrong way to look at it. There is an abundance out there. The clients I'm going to be seeing in the next 10 or 15 years are still in primary school. As a coach, when you're good, you know you're good, so are you going to be intimidated by anyone? Others might operate from that sort of fear, but I am never going to.

When I first started, I knew what my limitations were, but I was honest enough and humble enough to acknowledge that I needed to improve. I challenged myself and took responsibility for educating myself. In doing that, I established a mindset, a belief system and, more importantly, habitual behaviours that led me to fall in love with continual education and learning.

Keep seeking improvement

Once you've recognised your limitations, find experts to model yourself on. I went out and sought the best. I first started doing that when I was competing in Strongman, and later I started doing it for my coaching.

Initially, it manifested itself in the gym. The moment that I became one of the strongest in there, I got out. Why? Because I knew that I needed to grow, and that meant I had to go somewhere else where I was vulnerable again, where I was a small fish, where I could learn.

You have to be able to expose yourself to vulnerability. There are so many people who just don't want to be vulnerable and who go to extremes to protect themselves from that feeling. It's vital to investigate that vulnerability. That is where the gold is sometimes.

As a coach, you should be constantly seeking improvement. Nietzsche said that we have two options: we can go into nihilism because everything's absurd, or we can challenge ourselves to recreate our own values and become the best possible version of ourselves. The second option is exactly the mindset and the principles that I use in working with my clients. I take the approach that we've been given the gift of life, and with that we have a responsibility to be the best we can be and all we can be.

I spend a lot of time reading and I work hard. The more you learn, the more you want to continue to build that habit of investigation.

I would say that most people perceive me as an expert in my field. How I perceive myself is that I've got so much more to learn. To a certain point, that's probably a reflection of some of my belief systems that I'm working on, which is part of the reason why I'm doing my degree.

First seek to understand

We all have unconscious bias. One of the most important things for me as a coach is putting myself in a mindset where I can believe the things that my clients believe, in order to better understand them. People are quick to jump to conclusions without putting on other people's beliefs for a moment and trying to understand their perspective.

To truly go to that level of consciousness, you have to have some real training and a strong sense of self-belief and self-respect, and very few people will get to that.

This approach was pioneered by the American psychologist Carl Rogers, who to my mind was one of the greatest therapists. He had a very humanistic, non-judgemental approach to therapy, which led him to develop what is known as person-centred therapy. Rogers realised that it was important to allow clients to deal with the things they deemed important – not what the coach or therapist thought was important. I recommend anyone thinking about getting into coaching investigates his work further.

Be a do-it-now person

One of the things my first coach Clive would harp on about was, 'You've got to put a stop to putting things off.'

I turned that into an affirmation for myself: 'You must be a do-it-now person.'

That's important, because it prompts you to take immediate action to carry out tasks that you might otherwise be tempted to put off.

Don't be afraid to be different

When it comes to presenting seminars, my idols are Jim Rohn, who was a great motivational speaker, and Billy Connolly, because there's real power in being able to make people laugh. As a result, when I run a seminar, I've got to hit the three Es: it's got to be entertaining, educational and empowering.

Sometimes I think the challenge is that I haven't gone through the traditional channels and I'm self-taught. But somehow, I have a way of communicating with people. I have these incredible in-depth conversations.

When I run a seminar, I'll have been given a brief and I'll have a structure or plan in place, but I can read an audience and work from there. I don't have a prepared speech or run off a visual presentation. My years of experience mean that I am able to trust the process and have confidence in myself to deliver what's needed.

One night, I did a seminar for a big hardware chain. There were about 500–600 people there. I was on stage, and 30 seconds into it, I said, 'Hey, guys, before we start, we all know that there's an important game on tonight. Those who know know.' That game was a State of Origin match.

At this point, none of them had any clue who I was. They'd had six people come and speak during the day, so I was just another person talking for most of them. They were probably thinking, 'Here we go … motivation … whatever …'

I continued, 'I just want to get a gauge of the room. How many of you are Queensland fans?'

All these people cheered, while the New South Wales fans groaned.

'Now, I want all you Queensland fans to stand up.'

They all stood up and looked quite proud of themselves.

Then I said, 'Right, now you can piss off, the lot of you, you pack of losers!'

There was absolute uproar.

I carried on and ran the seminar, which everyone enjoyed.

Afterwards, as they were leaving, a whole lot of the guys gave me a hard time about being a New South Wales fan. I gave it straight back. It was brilliant. I knew they'd listened to every word I'd said, despite probably having started out wishing they were anywhere but at some motivational talk.

It wasn't all jokes though, and I knew I'd done some seriously good work that night when this lovely Māori woman came up to me and said, 'Dave, your message really resonated with me.' Then she told me some of her story.

I started getting a bit emotional, which often happens when people give me that sort of feedback. As I stood there, teary-eyed, she took off her pounamu and put it around my neck, saying, 'You've got to understand the importance of this. You can't buy one of these. They have to be gifted to you, and I want to gift this to you.'

I burst into tears. It was so cool. I still get little messages from people who were there that night. That means so much to me.

My job is to create superstars, not become one

I ran a seminar for the Navy. One of the guys said, 'We want to take you out for lunch at the officers' mess.'

I said, 'If you don't mind, I'd rather go to the main mess.' I don't feel like I'm special and need to have special treatment. I'm just an average guy.

I love being acknowledged and I have a real sense of pride when people talk about working with me, but would I want that in my mind all the time? No. I'm happy working in the background and making sure the people who work with me achieve what they want.

Build humble confidence

Leaders build leaders. I've heard coaches talk about leaders having to be humble. That depends on your definition of humility. Leaders need to be assertive and confident.

I've been humble on my journey. I've been very keen to learn. I've been respectful of that. I've sought the very best in the field, and I'm very blessed to have had some great mentors and coaches. Through that process I've built what I call humble confidence, while not losing sight of the importance of being assertive. It sounds counter intuitive. People say that they love the fact that I've got humble confidence, but I can also be very assertive when it's required. There's a time to be humble, and there is a time to be assertive.

I get a real sense of satisfaction when I get acknowledged. I'm humble in the sense that I'm not afraid to blow my own trumpet when it's necessary, but I don't do it week in and week out.

Give back

I've always said that the true purpose of a leader is to build other leaders. That's why I coach coaches. I do it because I want to help maintain the integrity of the industry and because I get a real kick out of seeing these people succeed. We shouldn't lose sight of the importance of giving something back once you're in a position to do so.

I absolutely trust that the cream always rises to the top. There are some exceptional coaches out there, wonderful people who make incredible sacrifices for their craft and for their clients. These people have real passion for what they do and that shines.

EPILOGUE

If I died today, I'd be fulfilled. I'm very proud of what I've done and I'm very satisfied with what I've achieved. Is there more to do? Absolutely! But I'm proud of the fact that I've identified what I wanted and designed my life around that. I've achieved a lot more than I ever imagined I would as the young Dave.

The Dave from back then, who was convinced he was thick and the best he'd ever do was working as a printer, would be pretty surprised to find out where I've ended up. Everyone has a different definition of success. For me, that's a happy marriage, children I'm proud of, work I love and never having to set an alarm. I've achieved all of those things, but there's always more to do.

When I break it down to a simple structure, there have been three key questions in my life I've had to answer.

First – how do I overcome the bullying? The solution was to become the biggest, strongest motherf*cker I could be.

Second – if I'm going to do this for a job, how do I overcome my fear of public speaking? I had to just face my fear and get up there and do it. Now I get paid to get up there and talk – and I love it.

Getting over those two things has been 30 years in the making.

The last frontier for me was the biggest of them all – overcoming my fear of academia. My track record? Nothing. I'd had pretty much no education. Overcoming that is what I'm moving towards right now, and that really excites me. I'm going to extract as much out of it as possible.

I've got two years until I've finished my university degrees. I'm already thinking about what I'll do once they're done. I've decided I'll take a break, go overseas to see the world and visit my daughter in London.

In terms of my coaching, that motivation to continue comes from the fact that I'm doing some of my best work now. After 30 years, I'm still on this incredible journey of getting better and better. My biggest buzz comes when a client leaves and I know they're armed with a toolbox of strategies and beliefs that will serve them for the rest of their lives. I see the change in the way they represent themselves, in their language and in their physiology. That makes me want to keep learning, evolving and growing.

Some people might say, 'You're a bit too critical of yourself.'

Well, maybe I am, but there's nothing wrong with that. I'm OK with being critical of myself without disempowering myself. I'm critical because I demand more of and for myself. That's a continuation that will never stop.

If you stop doing those things, you become vulnerable. I love the fact that my development is an ongoing thing, physically at first and now intellectually. I just want to extract as much as I can out of life, because you never know when it's going to finish.

For Jo and me, our ultimate goal is to be living by the beach, waking to the sound of the waves, then taking a walk along the beach with the dogs before coming back for breakfast and coffee. I'll have a couple of clients in the morning, then I'll go to the gym. In the afternoon, I'll research, study and read. Maybe we'll have the grandchildren over (no pressure though, kids!). I don't care about Lamborghinis and expensive watches; I just care about being able to enjoy life for what it is.

We all need to appreciate magic moments when they happen. I had one recently. It was my son Mitchell's 21st birthday and the four of us went down to Queenstown.

One evening, after a lovely dinner, we all sat outside around an open fire. It was amazing. We just talked and laughed for hours.

Gazing up at the night sky, Mitchell said, 'Dad, it doesn't get much better than this, eh?'

It really doesn't.

Life is about creating magical moments, so remember that you are the most incredibly exciting project you'll ever work on. If everyone took personal responsibility to improve, this world would be a better place, we'd have a better understanding of each other and we could live with a lot more harmony.

ENDNOTES

1 Doran, GT, 'There's a S.M.A.R.T. way to write management's goals and objectives', *Management Review*, 1981, 70 (11): 35–36.
2. 'Youth in Search for Meaning', St Michael's College, University of Toronto, Ontario, Canada, 1972. www.youtube.com/watch?v=fD1512_XJEw&t=9s
3. Dubber, Rebecca, 'Teenager Tupou finds silver lining in the pool', Newsroom, 15 September 2019. www.newsroom.co.nz/2019/09/15/teenager-tupou-finds-silver-lining-in-the-pool
4. Tayag, Yasmin, 'Six NASA Astronauts Describe the Moment in Space when "Everything Changed"', *Inverse*, 28 March 2018. www.inverse.com/article/42902-nasa-astronauts-describe-overview-effect-everything-changed
5. Hinton, Marc, 'Bouncing back: Alex Pledger set for storybook post-cancer NBL return for Sharks', Stuff, 9 March 2023. www.stuff.co.nz/sport/basketball/300873264/bouncing-back-alex-pledger-set-for-storybook-postcancer-nbl-return-for-sharks